William Gilbert Cassard, Everett Bird Mero

Battleship Indiana, and her part in the Spanish-American War

William Gilbert Cassard, Everett Bird Mero

Battleship Indiana, and her part in the Spanish-American War

ISBN/EAN: 9783337304881

Printed in Europe, USA, Canada, Australia, Japan

Cover: Foto ©ninafisch / pixelio.de

More available books at **www.hansebooks.com**

BATTLESHIP INDIANA

AND HER PART IN THE SPANISH-AMERICAN WAR

ILLUSTRATED FROM PHOTOGRAPHS AND ORIGINAL SKETCHES MADE DURING THE WAR-TIME. TOGETHER WITH THE ANNUAL REPORT OF THE COMMANDING OFFICER, WAR REPORTS, AND SOME GENERAL INFORMATION CONCERNING THE INDIANA. ALSO, A LIST OF THE OFFICERS AND ENLISTED MEN WHO SERVED ON BOARD THE SHIP DURING THE MONTHS OF ACTIVE HOSTILITIES

EDITED BY
WILLIAM G. CASSARD, U.S.N.
CHAPLAIN OF THE U. S. S. INDIANA

COMPILED AND PUBLISHED FOR
THE INDIANA SHIP'S COMPANY

BY EVERETT B. MERO, CHIEF YEOMAN, U.S.N.

NEW YORK, 1898

To meet the expressed wishes of officers and enlisted men of the United States Battleship Indiana for some permanent record of the ship's doings in the war between the United States and Spain, 1898, this small book has been prepared, with the hope that it may, to some extent, answer that purpose.

The illustrations are taken, for the most part, from a series of photographs made by Chaplain Cassard of the Indiana.

These photographs have a war history of their own. Most of them were negatives stored in the stateroom of the Chaplain at the time the Spanish shell came on board and exploded, as told in Chapter Seven. When he entered his room after the explosion he found his camera, film rolls, etc., mingled with the rest of the contents of his room in the middle of the floor in four inches of water. Some of the undeveloped films were exposed to the rays of electric light and that accounts for the peculiar appearance of several of the illustrations in this volume, although it adds interest to them.

For the benefit of friends of the ship ashore a small amount of space is devoted to general information concerning the vessel.

CONTENTS

CHAPTER I

Events of the Year.—The Annual Report of the Commanding Officer of the Battleship Indiana, giving the Official Story of One Year in Peace and in War. (By Captain Henry C. Taylor.) . . 1

CHAPTER II

Getting Ready for Hostilities.—A Running Story of the Indiana's Preparations for War, her Conduct under Fire, and a Word Picture of Events on Board in Action. (By Chief Yeoman Everett B. Mero.) 29

CHAPTER III

Memorable July Third.—The Part taken by the Indiana in the Exciting and Historical Events of that Day at Santiago. Her Eager Pursuit of a Supposed Spanish Battleship. The Work of Mercy following the Battle. Official Orders of Congratulation. The Return North. (By Chaplain William G. Cassard.) . . . 42

CHAPTER IV

Extracts from the Log of the Indiana.—May 4th, 5th, 11th, 12th; June 22d; July 2d, 3d, 4th, 5th, 10th, 11th 72

CHAPTER V

The Gun-fire.—Report to the Bureau of Ordnance of Ammunition expended in the Several Actions of the War. (By Lieutenant Samuel P. Comly.) 97

CHAPTER VI

The Marine Guard.—Report to the Colonel Commandant, U. S. Marine Corps, telling the Story of the Indiana's Marines in Battle. (By Captain Littleton W. T. Waller.) 105

CHAPTER VII

Story of the Punch Bowl.—How it Obtained its Battle Scar. Also, Details of the Havoc caused by the Explosion of One 8-inch Shell from a Spanish Mortar Battery. (By Chaplain W. G. Cassard.) 111

CHAPTER VIII

Ship's Company and Prizes of War.—List of the Officers, Crew, and Marines on Board the Indiana at the Time of the Action of July 3d, 1898, off Santiago de Cuba; also, the Prize Vessels in Whose Capture the Indiana was Specially Concerned. The War Volunteers. 119

CHAPTER IX

The Internal Mechanism.—Miscellaneous Information about the Indiana, showing the Varied Industries carried on on Board a Battleship, the Guns and their Ammunition, etc. . . . 130

CHAPTER X

Newspaper Notices.—Press Mention of the Indiana and Matters concerning the Ship. Some Words in Appreciation of Attention Received 138

ILLUSTRATIONS

CAPTAIN HENRY C. TAYLOR . . *Frontispiece*	
"He fought in the good old way."	
	PAGE
THE INDIANA	vi
"Of all the ships of the Navy . . . perhaps none saw more service than did the United States battleship Indiana."	
THE INDIANA AS SHE APPEARED IN DRY DOCK AT NEW YORK NAVY YARD, OCTOBER, 1898	xiv
PLAN SHOWING THE FORMATION OF THE NAVAL FLEET AND THE TRANSPORTS WITH GENERAL SHAFTER'S ARMY, JUNE, 1898 .	3
BOMBARDMENT OF SAN JUAN DE PUERTO RICO ON MAY 12TH— SHOWING THE FORMATION AND MOVEMENTS OF THE SHIPS .	7
OFFICERS IN "BATTLE UNIFORM" (SAN JUAN)	11
CAPTAIN TAYLOR OF THE INDIANA AND COMMANDER MCCALLA OF THE MARBLEHEAD HAVE A CONSULTATION WITH A CUBAN COLONEL CONCERNING APPROACH TO DAIQUIRI WITH THE TRANSPORTS	15
THE CUBAN COLONEL LEAVES THE SHIP, THE SIDE MANNED AND THE CAPTAIN AND OFFICER OF THE DECK HENDERSON DOING THE HONORS	19
GENERAL SHAFTER'S ARMY BEING TRANSPORTED TO CUBA, THE INDIANA SENIOR SHIP, AND CAPTAIN TAYLOR IN COMMAND .	23
THE INDIANA IN ACTION, JULY 3D	27
PLAN SHOWING THE FORMATION OF THE FIRST FLEET GOING TO BLOCKADE HAVANA AT THE OUTBREAK OF THE WAR . .	33
JUST AFTER THE SAN JUAN DE PUERTO RICO ACTION—PAYMASTER FRAZER, GUNNER MALLERY, MASTER-AT-ARMS KEATING, AND SOME OF THE "MEN BEHIND THE GUNS"	37
"AS THE CREW GATHERED . . . ON THE TOP OF THE TURRETS"	39
PLAN SHOWING THE MOVEMENTS OF THE INDIANA AND THE OTHER SHIPS IN THE BATTLE OF JULY 3D . . . . *facing*	44
"IT WAS DURING A LULL AT THE CLOSE OF THE BATTLE"	47

	PAGE
AUSTRIAN CRUISER KAISERIN MARIA THERESA	53

"We saw a string of international signals run up from the signal yard-arm."

SPANISH PRISONERS ON BOARD THE INDIANA	57

"It was noticeable that they donned the uniform of Uncle Sam with calm philosophy and without a word of protest."

ANOTHER VIEW OF THE SPANISH PRISONERS ON BOARD THE INDIANA	61
"TWO BURNING, SMOKING WRECKS OF WHAT WERE A LITTLE WHILE BEFORE THE SPANISH SHIPS MARIA TERESA AND OQUENDO"	65
VIEW OF THE MARIA TERESA'S QUARTER-DECK, STARBOARD SIDE, AFTER THE BATTLE	69
THE BAND	75

Composed of musically inclined members of the ship's company, this organization made much pleasure for all hands during the sometimes monotonous days of inactive war duty.

THE LANDING OF TROOPS AT DAIQUIRI—THE NEW ORLEANS IN THE CENTRE OF THE SCENE	79
SCENE OF THE BOMBARDMENT OF SANTIAGO ON JULY 2D	83
THE INDIANA'S BATTLE FLAGS AS THEY FLEW IN THE BREEZES BEFORE SANTIAGO DE CUBA, JULY 4, 1898	87
ONE OF THE PENETRATED DECK, OR FLASH, PLATES OF THE INDIANA, HIT BY SPANISH SHELL, JULY 4TH	91
A VIEW OF THE DECK BEAMS OF THE MARIA TERESA AFTER THE FIRE CAUSED BY THE SHELLS OF THE INDIANA AND THE OTHER SHIPS HAD BURNED AWAY ALL THE WOODWORK	95
VIEW OF THE PORT QUARTER-DECK OF THE MARIA TERESA	101
CAPTAIN LITTLETON W. T. WALLER, COMMANDING MARINE GUARD OF THE INDIANA, CAPTURES TWO PRIZES	107
THE PUNCH BOWL—SHOWING DENT MADE BY FRAGMENT OF SHELL, AND THE FRAGMENT MOUNTED	113
THE SOCAPA BATTERY SHELL AS IT CAME THROUGH THE INDIANA'S QUARTER-DECK AT MIDNIGHT ON THE FOURTH OF JULY	117
ASSISTANT ENGINEER GARRISON INTERESTS TWO OF THE INDIANA'S MASCOTS WHILE THE CHAPLAIN TAKES A "SNAP"	123
WAR TROPHIES AND SCENES ABOARD SHIP	133
HOW THE VISITORS FLOODED THE SHIPS ON THEIR RETURN FROM THE VICTORIES OF PUERTO RICO AND CUBA	141

THE INDIANA

As she appeared in dry-dock at New York Navy Yard in October, 1898

INTRODUCTION

A DESIRE on the part of the crew to preserve some record of the services of a man-of-war performed during a stirring period in the country's history is natural and commendable. When, as in the case of the Indiana, the services have been valuable and have assisted in bringing to a triumphant close a war undertaken for the high and noble purpose of avenging affronts to the nation and bringing aid to suffering peoples living near our shores, this praiseworthy desire deserves to be recognized.

In the case of a vessel whose officers and crew are frequently being changed, such a record should be prepared soon after the events have occurred, and to be full in detail must be a compilation of official documents and personal description. This has been undertaken in the case of the Indiana by certain of the officers and crew; and the work of Chaplain Cassard in editing and of Chief Yeoman Mero in compiling and publishing are specially commendable.

The Indiana's record has special interest on account of her uninterrupted presence at the scene of hostilities. While drilling and preparing for war at Tortugas and off Key West she heard, on the 15th of February, of the destruction of the Maine, and the news of the declaration of war which followed in April came to men thoroughly ready for war and eager for revenge. Some ships went north to join other squadrons, but the Indiana remained close at the front and in the heart of the scene of war from January to August, when she sailed from Guantanamo for home.

The blockade of Havana and the campaign against Puerto Rico, the series of events which brought about the important duty of convoying General Shafter's army to Santiago—a work of much difficulty resulting in complete success; the blockade of Santiago and the bombardments connected therewith, culminating in the battle of the 3d of July with Cervera's squadron; the affair of the Mercedes and the long-range bombardment of the city of Santiago—all these incidents, crowded into a short space of time, gave to the Indiana a fulness of fighting experience and a completeness of record which was the fortune of but few vessels in the war.

Throughout this period the readiness of the ship for service of all kinds, and the cheerful eagerness of the officers and crew for work or fighting, indicated the degree of efficiency she had attained and of which all persons connected with the Indiana may well be proud. For them and their families, as well as for those citizens of the State of Indiana who have always evinced an eager and generous interest in the ship and sympathy with it in its triumphs, this book is published, with the hope that it may be satisfactory to all who wish to know the details of the battleship Indiana's part during the war with Spain.

H. C. Taylor
Captain U. S. Navy
Comdg. Battleship "Indiana"

NAVY YARD, NEW YORK,
December, 1898.

THE BATTLESHIP INDIANA

AND HER PART IN THE SPANISH-AMERICAN WAR

CHAPTER I

EVENTS OF THE YEAR

The Annual Report of the Commanding Officer of the Indiana, giving the Official Story of One Year in Peace and War.

U. S. S. INDIANA, *First Rate*,
NEW YORK, *September* 10, 1898.

Sir: I have the honor to report the operations of the Indiana under my command from July 1, 1897, to August 20, 1898.

The beginning of the year found us at the Brooklyn Navy Yard, undergoing slight repairs, the time and money allowed not being sufficient for the general overhauling of engines and boilers we needed, and the failure of the dry-dock preventing our placing the bilge keels which had been strongly recommended.

We were ordered away from the Navy Yard to join Admiral Sicard's squadron, preparing for sea at Tompkinsville, and we left the yard July 27, 1897, and arrived at Tompkinsville the same day, saluting the flag of Rear-Admiral Miller in the Brooklyn at that anchorage. On July 29th Rear-Admiral Sicard arrived in his flagship New York, and on August 2d the squadron sailed, arriving in Newport on August 3d, and participating in the *fêtes* celebrated there on August 4th. The Indiana, leaving the squadron there, sailed August 5th for Halifax, it having been decided by the Department that we should have a hurried docking there in order to clean the bottom. We arrived in Halifax, August 7th, and found Naval Constructor Bowles awaiting us, I having requested the Department that a constructor be sent there to superintend the preparation of the dock and all technical details of our docking and undocking. It was arranged between him, the dockmaster, and myself that Mr. Bowles should take charge of the work in the same manner as is customary at our navy yards, and the ship was docked at 7.10 A.M. August 12th.

When the pumping of the dock had lowered the water a few feet, a watch was set in the double bottoms to discover any signs of straining as the weight of the ship was taken on the blocks. When the water was out of the dock a slight buckling was observed in double bottom compartments from frame No. 22 to frame No. 32, being most marked at frame No. 29, and decreasing forward and abaft that frame. Additional blocking was used under those portions of the ship's bottom, and preparations made to flood the dock. This proved unnecessary, however, and the work of cleaning and painting bottom proceeded, the paint used being as follows: McInnes Anti-Corrosive Paint and Anti-Fouling Paint. At 10.10 A.M. August 16th the ship left the dock, and after coaling sailed for Bar Harbor.

The British officials showed us much attention, Governor Daly, General Montgomery Moore, and Vice-Admiral Sir James Erskine giving entertainments in our honor. The citizens, led by the Mayor, showed cordial eagerness to be polite, and several thousands of people visited the ship when in dock. The Vice-Admiral expressed an admiration for the ship, but feared that she was too heavily armed to be serviceable in rough weather.

A few hours out from Halifax we had target practice, simulating conditions of actual battle, and manœuvring the ship from the conning tower.

During a foggy night off Cape Sable, we narrowly escaped running down several schooners of a large fishing fleet which we passed through.

We arrived in Bar Harbor August 20th, the Admiral with the rest of the squadron coming in August 24th. The weather there is good at this season and the climate healthful, and some of the neighboring portions of the coast, such as Blue Hill Bay, would, I believe, be excellent localities for the fleet drills and exercises in August and September.

Leaving Bar Harbor, August 31st, the squadron proceeded with-

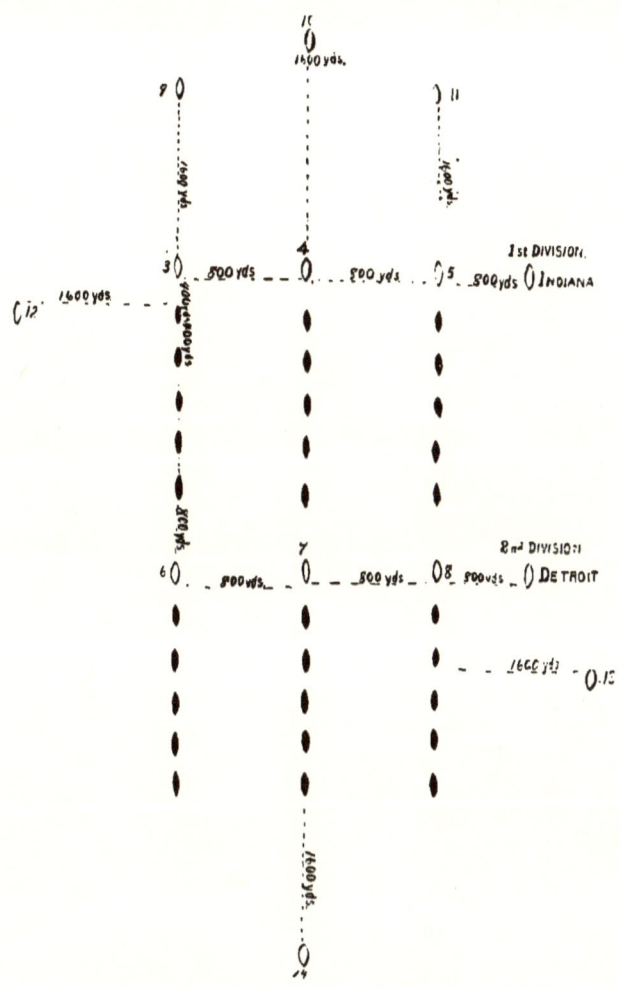

PLAN SHOWING THE FORMATION OF THE NAVAL FLEET AND THE TRANSPORTS WITH GENERAL SHAFTER'S ARMY, JUNE, 1898

(This formation was varied according to circumstances and was not always as here shown)

KEY TO NUMBERS ON PLAN

1. Indiana.
2. Detroit.
3. Annapolis.
4. Castine.
5. Helena.
6. Bancroft.
7. Manning.
8. Hornet.
9. Osceola.
10. Wompatuck.
11. Dupont.
12. Pompey.
13. Eagle.
Despatch boats Ericsson and Rodgers.

out incident to the Southern drill ground off the Chesapeake, and exercised there at manœuvres and target practice until September 4th, when we entered Hampton Roads, and having coaled the ships proceeded, September 27th, to Yorktown for boat exercises and landing drills. Leaving Yorktown October 4th, and anchoring in Chesapeake Bay, we proceeded thence, on October 5th, to the drill ground and continued the exercises.

On the night of October 9th, in obedience to signal, the Indiana left the squadron and anchored in Hampton Roads under orders to await there the Department's instructions, and to keep ready for instant departure. Having coaled at Newport News, I received the Department's permission to await its orders at Yorktown, and reaching there October 21st constructed a rifle range on shore and exercised at rifle, boat, gun, and sub-calibre practice for fifteen days. We left Yorktown November 9th, and proceeded to the drill ground for ship-handling practice, returning to Hampton Roads November 11th, and again awaited the Department's instructions, until the Admiral arrived on December 21st.

During this period such overhauling to machinery as could be carried on was done, but the obligation to keep constantly ready for immediate sailing upon receipt of Department's order made any disabling of machinery, for the purpose of thorough repair, contrary to the spirit of my instructions.

On January 7th the commanding officer was granted sick leave, and on January 16th the Indiana sailed with the squadron for the Gulf of Mexico. On the passage the boiler tubes began to give out in such numbers that the ship's speed was impaired, and upon arriving at Tortugas it was decided to retube the boilers, and for that purpose a set of new tubes of iron was sent to Tortugas with which to replace the old ones, which were of steel.

The commanding officer returned from sick leave February 14th. The news of the destruction of the Maine reached Admiral Sicard at Dry Tortugas on the morning of February 16th, and at a council of his captains he determined to proceed to Key West, leaving the remainder of his squadron in Tortugas. The Indiana lay there until March 21st, occupying the time in retubing and cleaning boilers, overhauling the machinery, now in much need of repairs, and training the crew to a high point of efficiency for war. Patrol boats were used to guard the entrance through the reef, and a vigilance was observed which thoroughly trained officers and crew for war.

The time spent at the Dry Tortugas was of great benefit to the ship's company in preparing them for the conditions of actual war, and to that period and its work is largely attributable the excellent marksmanship displayed by the crew and officers, rising to its greatest value in the action of July 3d. To the same cause may be in great part assigned the coolness and readiness, the entire absence of all confusion, so noticeable throughout the ship's company in the various engagements of this war.

Leaving Dry Tortugas, March 21st, the Indiana anchored outside the reef at Key West to eastward of Sand Key Light. At this place we finished the retubing of the boilers on April 1st, and on April 2d went outside for a few hours' trial of the engines and boilers and to fire a few shots at a target. The boiler tubes proved to be in order, and no special defect was observed, but the loss of steam around pistons and through leaky valves was found to be so great that a speed of nine knots for cruising and of ten and a half for battle was the most we could expect to attain. The guns and mounts were very satisfactory in their workings. The drills and vigilant watchfulness continued during our stay here, and added their part to the efficiency manifested by the ship's company during the war.

On March 26th Admiral Sicard, having been invalided by Medical Board, was relieved in command of the squadron by Captain Sampson. On April 20th the Indiana was ordered to Dry Tortugas for coal, and having coaled returned to Key West, arriving there at daylight of April 22d; and finding that war had been declared against Spain and that the fleet was under way for Havana, we joined the column in obedience to signal without anchoring, and proceeded off Havana, where we patrolled with the fleet for several days and established the blockade of that port.

It had been previously arranged that the Indiana should go as senior ship of a small force to cut telegraph cables and reconnoitre along the east and south coasts of Cuba; and in pursuance of this plan I was notified by the Commander-in-Chief to pro-

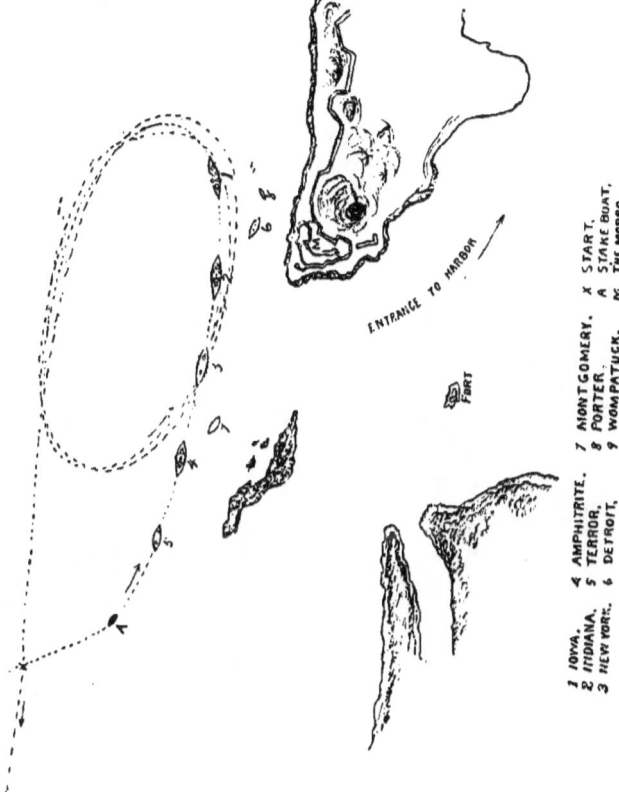

BOMBARDMENT OF SAN JUAN DE PUERTO RICO, MAY 12, 1898

Showing the movements of the ships engaged—positions are shown as in first passage of the Spanish batteries

(Drawn by Private N. J. Hurd, U.S.M.C., U. S. S. Indiana, from memory and suggestions from the Captain and officers of the Indiana)

ceed on this expedition. I left the blockade therefore on the 26th and proceeded to Tortugas for coal; while there I received notice of a telegram from Secretary Long to the Commander-in-Chief, directing him not to cut any cables. Having coaled and reached the Sand Cay anchorage near Key West, I awaited further instructions, and when none were received I telegraphed the Department as follows: " Shall Indiana, Detroit, and auxiliaries drag for cable off Santiago de Cuba and Guantanamo and destroy it?" the Department's reply being as follows: " Not to cut cables until further orders." I therefore proceeded, under the Commander-in-Chief's orders, in case of the Department's telegraph being of that nature, to Havana and resumed blockade.

On the 1st of May, news having been received of the departure of Admiral Cervera's squadron from the Cape Verdes for the West Indies, the Indiana proceeded to Key West and coaled ship, and on May 3d returned to the blockade, and on May 4th proceeded with the Commander-in-Chief and squadron to the eastward. The lack of thorough navy-yard work on this ship now became very marked, and the effort to maintain ten knots caused serious defects to appear in engines and boilers, culminating on May 6th off Cape Haitien in a slight bulging of crown sheets in several furnaces, and a consequent further reduction of steam pressure carried and of speed. Continuing the squadron's movement to the eastward, we arrived off San Juan de Puerto Rico before daybreak on May 12th and formed for attack, the principal column being Iowa leading, with Commander-in-Chief's flag temporarily carried, Indiana, New York, Amphitrite, Terror; the Detroit and Montgomery were used as flankers and guides in the attack.

At 5.20 stood in for the entrance of the harbor of San Juan, and reaching a point marked by boat A, turned to eastward and steered for a point B, marked by the Detroit, and thence to the northward and westward until out of range. This round was made three times, the firing continuing from A to B.

We opened fire, following the movements of the flagship, at daylight, and continued the firing during the three passages made in front of the forts. The morning was dull and the mist hung low, to which was added the smoke of our guns and of the enemy's, obscuring our aim to a serious degree, and forcing us to reserve our fire or to waste ammunition without obtaining results. We therefore fired a comparatively small number of projectiles (one hundred and eighty-seven), of which those in the first round did less execution than those in the latter two, serving as test shots for the range, and resulting finally in very effective shooting on the second and third passages before the forts. The enemy also, surprised only for a moment, had gathered to their guns by this time and replied with spirit during the two latter rounds, and the action now became brisk and vigorous on both sides.

Our fire was very effective. A few shots fell short in the first round, but the range being corrected, nearly every projectile told either against the Morro and battery adjacent or the houses of the town and small shipping of the port.

A French officer, Captain of the corvette Rigault de Genouilly, which was at the time in the port and in a very sheltered position, told me afterward that our fire had been very destructive to houses and batteries on shore, and to the spars and smokestacks of his ship, which was sheltered in its hull by the walls and houses of the dockyard intervening. This French captain, with whom I had a long conversation a few months afterward in Guantanamo, seemed much impressed with the effectiveness of the fire of our ships.

After the third round the Commander-in-Chief, in the Iowa, led out of action to the northward and westward a few miles, and after a council with some of his captains decided not to renew the action, the fighting already done having developed the fact that Cervera's squadron was not in San Juan, and his instructions being to seek him out and destroy his ships.

Returning to the westward, when off Puerto Plata, San Domingo, news was received by the Admiral that Cervera's squadron had reached Curaçoa, and sailed thence in a northwesterly direction, and that his ships were foul and not well supplied with coal. It was thought that Cervera would proceed from Curaçoa to one of four points—San Juan, Santiago de Cuba, Cienfuegos, or Havana. The first was thought unlikely because our fleet was in that vicinity; the second more probable, but still

unlikely, because our fleet was nearer there than the two last mentioned places. Cienfuegos and Havana were therefore thought the two ports to which Cervera would direct his course, and in consequence the squadron was ordered to hasten to Key West, and prepare to meet the enemy off Havana, while the flying squadron under Commodore Schley was directed to Cienfuegos.

What actually happened was that the enemy went to Santiago, moved thereto by scant coal supply and other reasons unknown to us.

Arriving at Key West on the 19th of May, the ship was coaled and proceeded off Havana, where she remained until news was received by the Commander-in-Chief that the Spanish squadron had gone to Santiago de Cuba, when we left the Havana blockade on May 23d and proceeded in company with the Commander-in-Chief, Commodore Watson, and a numerous squadron to the neighborhood of Cape Francese on the north coast of Cuba, where the Old Bahama Channel divides into the two channels Nicolas and Santarem. Here a strict watch was kept day and night to intercept the Spanish ships if they came eastward, and this position was held until certain news was received that Cervera's squadron was still in Santiago, and observed by Commodore Schley's, which had proceeded there from Cienfuegos, upon being convinced that the enemy was not in the latter port.

This being known, the Commander-in-Chief with two ships left for Santiago, and the Indiana was ordered to coal at Key West and occupy a few days in working at boiler repairs with the help of a force of mechanics sent there by the Department from the North.

Arriving at Key West May 30th the ship was coaled, and the boiler repairs were undertaken, but without success, the Key West force of mechanics not being yet equipped to work at such short notice. The opportunity was seized, however, to thoroughly clean and scale the boilers, and a force of divers, sent to Key West from the North, cleaned the ship's bottom quite thoroughly.

During this period I was notified that I would have charge of the convoy destined to take General Shafter's army from Tampa to Santiago de Cuba with the Indiana as senior ship, and was instructed by the Department through Commodore Remey, commanding the Key West Naval Base, to make all preparations for this duty. The time of repairs was therefore spent by the commanding officer of the Indiana in organizing the expedition, drafting the regulations, and indicating the precautions against attack from the small vessels of the enemy stationed in the bays and rivers along our route. In this work I was much assisted by Commander Hunker, who, being stationed at Tampa with the transports, carried out with much ability the details of the organization, and later took charge of the sailing from Tampa, turning over the convoy in excellent order to me at Dry Tortugas.

When about ready to sail, news was brought to Key West that a squadron of Spanish vessels had been seen the night before in that vicinity, and in consequence the Indiana was made senior ship of a reconnoissance of the channels and shores in that vicinity. The force placed under my command included the Detroit, Montgomery, Vesuvius, Bancroft. The Indiana, assisted by this force, made a thorough examination of the channels north of Cuba as far east as Cay Lobos, and returned to Key West on June 12th, having developed the fact that none of the enemy's vessels were in that locality.

The transports sailed from Tampa on June 14th, and on June 14th the Indiana sailed from Key West with her consorts and, anchoring off Dry Tortugas, awaited their arrival. On the evening of June 15th they were sighted approaching from the north, and on the following morning the Indiana hoisted the senior pennant and her commanding officer took command of the expedition. The transports were thirty-five in number, carrying about sixteen thousand men, under command of General Shafter, and were convoyed by a force of fifteen vessels, consisting of the Indiana, Detroit, Annapolis, Castine, Helena, Wasp, Wompatuck, Manning, Bancroft, Rodgers, Ericsson, Dupont, Osceola, Hornet, and Eagle.

The merchant vessels were formed in three columns, twelve in a column, with three men-of-war as column leaders. The Indiana took position upon the right of the leaders of columns. The rear division was placed under direction of Commander Dayton in the Detroit, which ship took position in the rear of

CAPTAIN TAYLOR OF THE INDIANA AND COMMANDER McCALLA OF THE MARBLEHEAD HAVE A CONSULTATION WITH A CUBAN COLONEL CONCERNING APPROACH TO DOGGERI WITH THE TRANSPORT.

the last ship of that division. Commander Clover in the Bancroft, assisted by some of the smaller vessels, was placed in command of the rear-guard, with directions to allow no transport to drop astern of him.

After the first day's steaming it became apparent that to keep the merchant ships closed up would result in a great lengthening of the voyage. It was in every way important that the transit of these troops should not be delayed unduly. I therefore, having arranged for the disabled or laggards to be cared for and protected by a sufficient force under Commander Clover, proceeded at a reasonable speed with the remainder of the convoy, communicating with the rear-guard from time to time by means of the small despatch-boats. This method proved entirely successful, and Commander Clover of the Bancroft was able to so hasten the slower transports in the rear that he arrived and joined my command within two hours after my arrival with the main body of the convoy off Santiago.

There were few incidents of note during the passage. Upon the first day out I visited the Seguranca, General Shafter's flagship, having saluted him with thirteen guns from the Indiana, and paid my respects and informed him of the general outline of the route proposed and the rules I had made. On the afternoon of the same day I sighted the broad pennant of Commodore Watson on the Montgomery, which I saluted with eleven guns, and received by signal from him congratulations upon the good order of my command. During the forenoon of the third day out Commander Hunker in the Annapolis, which led the northern column, reported the water shoaling, and signal was made to steer more to the southward in order to take greater distance from the edge of the Bahama Bank. The next forenoon, being through the Bahama Channel, and as General Shafter expressed a desire to communicate with some of his rear transports, I signalled the convoy to stop and to close up; and after a few hours' stay, and the rear ships having closed up, we continued on our course to the eastward.

The route had been planned so that we should pass close to Great Inagua Island, in order to take advantage of the smooth water under its lee if any ship should be disabled or in need of supplies. This precaution was amply justified by the result. One of the transports loaded with pack mules, a most important part of the army's equipment, ran short of water as we approached Inagua, and I was obliged to send her with escort of naval vessels into the smooth water to leeward of the island, and transfer water from another army transport to prevent the total loss of these valuable animals.

Turning the head of our column to the south at Inagua, and passing Cape Maysi and the south shore of Cuba at the distance of fifteen miles, I sent in a despatch-boat to Guantanamo at daylight and later to the fleet off Santiago to notify the Admiral of the arrival of the convoy. When we reached a point 15 miles south of Santiago entrance I received orders from Admiral Sampson to remain in charge of the convoy, and hold it off shore for a day or more until the place of landing the troops had been decided upon.

We remained stationary during the first night, but in the morning so much loss of position was noted from drifting, though several of our small vessels worked energetically to whip them in, that I determined to keep the squadron and convoy under way during the second night, more especially because the hour determined upon for landing at Daiquiri was so early as to leave no time to adjust any confusion in the convoy after daylight. I therefore determined to keep under way in three columns during the second night, and turning the heads of columns a few points at a time, to avoid the risk of breaking the formation, make a circle during the night and approach Daiquiri from the W. S. W. with the port column composed of transports first to land near the shore.

Requests from General Shafter for numerous changes of position among the ships of the convoy, not mentioned till the afternoon was well advanced, made the task difficult, and orders from the Commander-in-Chief to make certain disposition which did not reach me until nearly midnight, all combined to render the night's task difficult to perform. By the constant and untiring work of all the naval vessels, the evolution was, with slight exceptions, successfully carried out, and at daylight the heads of columns approached Daiquiri. The St. Louis and New Orleans

THE CUBAN COLONEL LEAVES THE SHIP, THE SIDE MANNED, THE CAPTAIN AND OFFICER OF THE DECK HENDERSON DOING THE HONORS, AND BOATSWAIN'S MATE CANAVAN PIPING HIM OVER THE SIDE.

were lying off that point of the coast, and as the Indiana approached, the Spanish flag on the blockhouse on the bluff overlooking the landing was hauled down, and the building at the wharf and other points in the village were set on fire by the enemy, who then withdrew.

My orders were imperative to bring the Indiana to the Santiago blockade as soon as the transports were in a position for landing their troops at Daiquiri. I therefore hauled down the senior officer's pennant as soon as a number of them had taken position, and steered for the Commander-in-Chief off Santiago. Arriving there at 8.25 A.M., the flagship signalled the Indiana at 9.25 A.M. to go close in.

Understanding this signal to mean us to engage the batteries, and the Texas being already engaged, we went in and opened fire, first on the eastern battery and the Morro, and later, having silenced them, we steamed to the westward across the entrance, engaging the Socapa and Punta Gorda batteries, until signalled to withdraw. These batteries engaged us briskly, and their projectiles, though generally wild, fell at times quite near us, one of them exploding under water so near the ship's side as to dish one of the bow plates.

After this affair the Indiana resumed her station on the blockade, and remained on that duty without incident of special note, outside the engagements, throughout the remainder of the campaign.

On the 30th of June the Indiana went to Guantanamo for coal, and while there learned that the fleet would attack the batteries at Santiago entrance on July 2d, and keep them engaged while the army, then in position in front of the city, would advance upon the intrenchments which protected the city. As this promised to be a serious action, the Indiana hastened her coaling and finished at midnight of July 1st.

At 4.30 A.M. on July 2d, the Indiana having just returned from Guantanamo, the flagship signalled the Indiana, " 'Take position between flagship and Oregon. We engage the batteries at daylight. Receive Mr. Staunton's call." In obedience to this signal took station assigned, cleared for action, and at 5.25 beat to general quarters. Closing inshore, a bombardment of the eastern batteries was commenced with the port battery, in obedience to General Signal No. 1. At 6.15 ceased firing, but commenced again at 6.31, having obtained permission to do so by signal.

* At 6.45 ceased firing and took position to westward, and at 7.05 opened fire with starboard battery upon Punta Gorda Battery. At 7.32 ceased firing and secured in obedience to signal. Many shots fell near us, but we were not struck.

When close under the Morro one of our shots appeared to carry away the Spanish flag there.

While the crew were at quarters at 9.37 A.M. of July 3d, preliminary to general muster, noted two guns fired from the Iowa and general signal, " Enemy's ships escaping," flying. At once cleared ship for action, and the crew were at the guns in a remarkably short time, the officers and men showing an alacrity that indicated clearly their pleasure at the opportunity offered them.

The Spanish squadron was seen emerging from the harbor, and in a few moments a general action ensued. The leading ship, which proved to be the Infanta Maria Teresa, flying the flag of Vice-Admiral Cervera, was followed by the other vessels of the squadron as follows: Vizcaya, Cristobal Colon, Oquendo, and the torpedo-boat destroyers Furor and Pluton. The enemy's vessels headed to the westward, and our ships headed in the same direction, keeping as nearly abreast of them as possible.

This ship fired on all of them as they came out one by one, and continued the action later by firing principally at the Maria Teresa, Oquendo, Furor, and Pluton. Several of our shells were seen to take effect on these vessels. Our secondary battery guns were directed principally on the destroyers, as also were the 6-inch guns. The destroyers were sunk through the agency of our guns and those of the Gloucester, which vessel had come up and engaged them close aboard.

The initial fire of all the Spanish ships was directed at this vessel, and although falling very close, only struck the ship twice, without injury to ship or crew.

Our ranges were obtained by stadimetre angles on the Morro as the ships emerged, and then by angles on the tops of the rear ships. The ranges were from forty-five hundred to two thousand

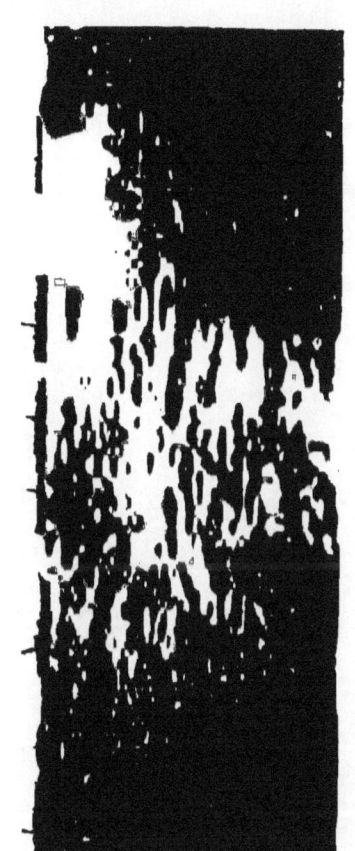

GENERAL SHAFTER'S ARMY BEING TRANSPORTED TO CUBA, THE INDIANA SENIOR SHIP OF THE NAVAL CONVOY, AND CAPTAIN TAYLOR IN COMMAND

yards, observed from the tops. From the bridge I could see that our shooting was excellent and showed its effects. One of our 13-inch shells was seen to enter the Maria Teresa under the quarter-deck and explode, and that ship was observed on fire very shortly after.

We were now very well satisfied with the results of persistent drilling of the battery and firing at a target, to which we had given such close attention during the twelve months preceding the war.

Our percentage of hits, judging by the eye, was very large, and the fire from this ship alone was so accurate and so sustained as to beat down the fire of the Spanish ships, and to inflict upon them injuries which greatly hastened the end of the battle. The Vizcaya, Oquendo, and Maria Teresa all felt the effects of our guns, the last two being under our fire until they surrendered.

The Pluton and the Furor, which were engaged by the Gloucester, were practically destroyed by the fire of the secondary battery of the Indiana.

About 10.15 observed the Maria Teresa and Oquendo on fire and heading for the beach, the fire from their guns having ceased. We now devoted our special attention to prevent the escape of the destroyers, which appeared to be more than a match for the Gloucester, she being the only small vessel near to engage them. They were seen to blow up, apparently hit by our 6-inch and 6-pounder guns. We now fired our large guns at the Vizcaya, which was at long range. She made for the beach soon after on fire and battery silenced. These ships hauled down their colors as they made for the beach. The Spanish flagship hoisted the white flag as she grounded.

We now ceased firing. The Colon was observed well over the western horizon closely pursued by the Brooklyn, Oregon, and Texas, off shore of her. The flagship New York, steaming full speed to the westward, as soon as the Vizcaya surrendered, signalled us, "Go back and guard entrance of harbor." Several explosions were observed on board the burning ships. At noon turned and stood to the eastward for our station in obedience to the above signal. Observed the Harvard and several transports standing to the westward.

About 12.30 the Resolute came within hail and informed us

by megaphone that a Spanish battleship was sighted to the eastward standing toward us. Later the Harvard passed, confirming the information, and adding that the ship was painted white. We made out the vessel ahead and stood for her with our guns bearing. She proved to be the Austrian armored cruiser Kaiserin Maria Theresa. She sent an officer on board and requested permission to enter the harbor. I referred him to the Commander-in-Chief. She then stood to the westward and we resumed our station.

After the destruction of Cervera's fleet the Indiana continued off Santiago de Cuba until July 17th, partaking in the long-range bombardment of that city on July 10th and 11th.

On the 17th the Indiana proceeded to Guantanamo Bay, where repairs were made upon her boilers by her own force and that of the Vulcan. At the same time all preparations were made for the voyage across the ocean with covering squadron with the Eastern Squadron. This being abandoned, the Indiana left Guantanamo with the flagship and other armored ships and arrived in New York on August 20th.

The ships there received a public welcome, the fleet steaming up to Grant's tomb, firing a salute in passing, and then returning to the anchorage off Tompkinsville.

Respectfully,
H. C. TAYLOR,
Captain U. S. Navy, Commanding U. S. S. Indiana.

THE SECRETARY OF THE NAVY,
  Washington, D. C.

CHAPTER II

GETTING READY FOR HOSTILITIES

A Running Story of the Indiana's Preparations for War, her Conduct under Fire, and a Word Picture of Events on Board in Action.

Of all the ships of the Navy that participated in the war campaign around the Cuban and Puerto Rican coasts, perhaps none saw more service than did the United States battleship Indiana. So it is quite appropriate that in telling the story of one ship's part in the war the Indiana should be taken as a typical subject.

There were other things in addition to fighting, battering down fortifications, and sinking enemy's fleets to occupy the attention of the officers and men on board ship during the short time the war lasted and the exciting weeks just preceding active hostilities, but they have been rather lost sight of by the general public in admiring contemplation of the great work with the guns, the spectacular finale of the whole affair. But thrown into the background by the more popular and more noisy demonstrations, these preliminary movements were nevertheless of great importance, and in one of the most important the Indiana was very actively concerned. This was the convoying of General Shafter's army from Tampa to Santiago under the command of Captain Taylor, with the Indiana as senior or flag ship. Upon the commanding officer of this ship devolved the task of arranging for the safe transportation of the sixteen thousand soldiers and the protection of the thirty-five transporting steamers from possible Spanish attack on the way.

That this was done so successfully, and the expedition landed at the prearranged destination on time and without a single mishap worthy of mention, reflects no little credit upon the naval officers who made the plans and carried them out. Captain Taylor was the recipient of many words of praise and much congratulation upon the safe and successful undertaking.

But to start at the beginning. Preparation for active warfare, which came according to expectations later, was begun by the Indiana, in common with all the other ships of the fleet, immediately after the destruction of the Maine. Among other things in the way of preparation was the removal of every particle of woodwork that could be dispensed with. This included all the wooden sheathing on the inside of the iron sides of the ship in the officers' rooms, the ward-room, and the cabin, as well as mess chests and many useful but not indispensable articles forward. The value of this wholesale tearing out of woodwork was shown in the case of the Indiana, when a Spanish shell from a shore mortar battery came down through the quarter-deck and set fire to what there was combustible in the ward-room passage-way. Had the usual amount of woodwork been there, the fire might have been a serious one instead of a small blaze extinguished with perfect ease.

Target practice was a feature of the Indiana's preparation, and continued a feature until there came a time to show the results at San Juan de Puerto Rico, and later on with Cervera's squadron at Santiago. Not only was the wisdom of the preparation shown by the accuracy of the gun-fire, but as well by the absence of confusion under fire, a very important element of actual war which the American possessed and the Spaniards seemed to lack—one explanation of the actual difference between the two forces when on paper their strength was more nearly equal.

The Indiana's first active war duty was in the blockade of Havana. Having been at Dry Tortugas, she steamed up to Sand Key light to join the rest of the fleet, only to find the other ships already on their way to Havana. So the Indiana fell into position, and Captain Evans of the Iowa megaphoned over to Captain Taylor: " War was declared yesterday; we are now going to blockade Havana." A hearty cheer went up from the men as they heard this long-expected and eagerly anticipated news.

An hour later and one of the fleet had taken a prize and fired the first hostile shot of the war in doing it.

Closing in on Havana, all preparations were made to return in kind any warm reception the guns of the forts might have waiting for the ships. The Indiana cleared for action, and her 13-inch turret guns were ready to do the work for which they were built.

Havana did not expect a fleet of American warships just at that time, as it developed afterward. From the deck of the Indiana the city could be seen in full enjoyment of life and gayety, streets and buildings brilliantly illuminated and thronged with people. When the approach of the American ships was discovered there was doubtless a hurried consultation of officials in the city, for it was not long before the lights began to disappear one by one. By means of a long glass the people in the streets could be seen hurrying either to the water front to verify rumors or hastening in the opposite direction toward their homes. It was not very long before the city was thoroughly aroused to dangers they knew not of, and darkness took the place of brilliancy throughout the city. But no shots were fired, and Havana was unharmed.

Nerve-wearing blockade duty continued with few incidents of importance until the news came of the approach of Admiral Cervera's squadron, about the only relief being the prospect of a cable-cutting expedition of which the Indiana was to be senior ship and Captain Taylor in command, but which was countermanded by orders from Washington just as the work was about to be begun.

Another item of interest about this time was the capturing of a prize, the Spanish ship Panama, by the Mangrove, assisted by the Indiana. It was on April 25th that the Panama fell a victim to these vessels, after a little persuasion in the shape of a plucky attack by the Mangrove and a 6-pounder shot across the steamer's bow fired by Boatswain Dowling of the Indiana. As the Spanish colors went down, a cheer that shook the ship went up from the battleship's decks, and there was a good-natured rivalry to get into the prize crew which was to go on board the Panama to take her into port. This prize crew was made up entirely of Indiana men, with Cadet Falconer in charge.*

Leaving the Havana blockade, the Indiana went with Admiral Sampson and his fleet in search of Cervera's ships, with the intention of engaging them in battle. It was thought they might have put into San Juan, and so to the Puerto Rican coast the fleet proceeded. Arriving there while the gray of dawn was creeping up from the east on the morning of May 12th, the fleet formed in line of battle, with the Indiana next to the Iowa, which was being used for the occasion as flagship. In anticipation of action, all hands were called aft and mustered on the quarter-deck. In a brief speech Captain Taylor addressed the men who were about to go into their first battle—a battle with, as it was supposed, the enemy's powerful fleet, who were about to give the great battleship her baptism of fire. He assured them of his confidence in their ability to bring credit to the flag under which they would fight, to the country, to the ship on which they were serving, and to themselves.

At signal from the flagship, the vessels closed in on San Juan at daylight and opened a fire to which the guns of the Spanish forts on shore made a spirited reply. Three times the ships steamed past the forts, maintaining a brisk fire all the time. The object of all this was to ascertain if Admiral Cervera was in the harbor with his fleet. It was soon demonstrated that he was not, so the American ships drew out of action, the Spanish gunners sending a few shots after the ships as they went to sea; but, like all the rest, these shots hit the water mostly. This bombardment was the first time under fire for the Indiana, and she acquitted herself with great credit. It was a demonstration of the benefits of being ready and a proof of the wisdom of the preliminary practice and maintenance of war-time precaution.

The next move in the chase after Cervera's elusive fleet took the Indiana to Key West, where she, with the fleet, was ordered to be ready to make a dash across to Havana to meet the Span-

---

* The men were: E. Brodd, Sea.; J. B. Hedenger, Sea.; P. Downey, O. S.; W. B. May, O. S.; A. F. Kelly, App.; Sergt. C. Schneider; Privates G. Colter, E. N. Hescock, A. Holmberg, A. Gunter, T. H. Jernigan, P. Maher, D. Looney, C. O. Seivers, W. O. Boyer, M. Brooks.

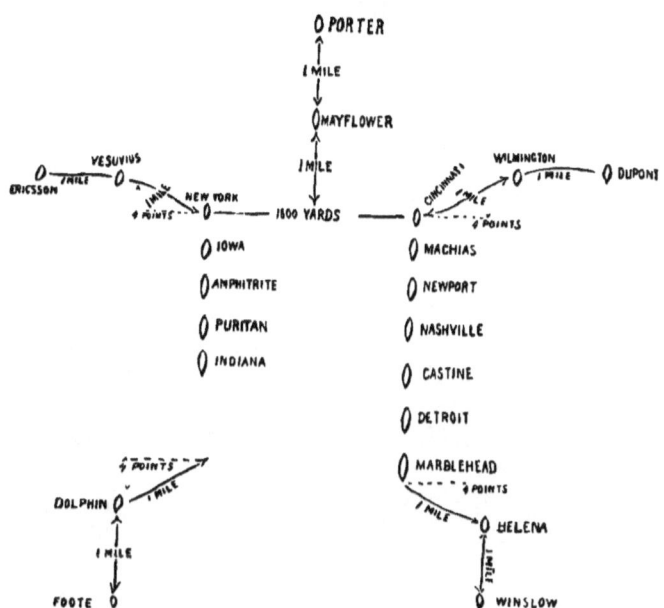

PLAN OF FORMATION OF FLEET ON THE WAY TO HAVANA, APRIL 23, 1898

Porter and Mayflower, advance scouts; Wilmington and Dupont, Vesuvius and Ericsson, flankers; Dolphin and Foote, Helena and Winslow, rear guard.

ish ships if they should come to that port. As everybody knows now they did not come, but went to Santiago de Cuba instead. So it became the fleet's duty to follow. The ships proceeded off the northwestern coast of Cuba, and there waited to head off the Spaniards if they came that way from Santiago. Nothing being seen of them, the fleet made the next move and closed in on Santiago. The Indiana did not accompany the fleet to Santiago, but went to Key West instead for slight repairs and coaling in anticipation of important convoy duty. It was while at this point that the army of invasion completed its preparations to sail, and the Indiana became senior ship of the naval convoying fleet. While the repairs on the Indiana were in progress her commanding officer was busy with the work of preparing for the expedition, the first movement of the sort in the history of the United States and one of the largest undertakings of its nature ever known.

When everything was apparently ready for the convoys and transports to sail, there came the alarming news of a Spanish fleet just outside, waiting to play havoc with the troops and the ships *en route*. The Indiana at once started out with several smaller vessels, and made a thorough three days' search of all the inlets and bays along the coast of Cuba to the north, as well as keeping a lookout on the open sea, but not an unfriendly craft of any sort could be discovered. Captain Taylor returned and so reported to the authorities.

Nothing further appearing to keep the troops back, and the navy being ready then, as at all times, the transports and convoys sailed the middle of June, the Indiana acting as flagship and being at the right of the long triple column of vessels, each of the columns being headed by a warship. To keep the ships closed up and at the same time not hasten unduly the slower ships was one of the tasks which Captain Taylor had to accomplish. It was done by maintaining a rear-guard under command of a competent naval officer, and so making certain that none of the transports dropped to the rear too far. Arriving at the destination on the south coast of Cuba on the morning of June 20th, Captain Taylor sent in a despatch-boat to Guantanamo and Santiago to notify the naval authorities there of the approach of the troops, and the following day his big fleet was off Daiquiri waiting to land. This was done two days later. As soon as the troopships were in position the Indiana proceeded to Santiago de Cuba and took her blockading station, and remained there until the destruction of Cervera's fleet and the fall of the city. She reached there at a few minutes after eight o'clock on the morning of June 22d, and inside of an hour was busily at work helping the Texas engage the eastern battery and the guns of the Morro. Their guns silenced, the Indiana opened fire on the next set of batteries, which happened to be the Socapa and Punta Gorda fortifications. The gunners of these batteries made things very lively for the Indiana and the Texas, the two ships engaged. As a rule the Spanish gunnery was of the usual sort and the hits were few, but narrow escapes were plenty. One shell came so near striking the Indiana that it exploded under water, just under the starboard bow, leaving its imprint in one of the bow-plates. A few feet more and there would have been a hole down through the forecastle similar to the one the same guns put in the quarter-deck a few days later.

The Indiana remained on blockade duty, leaving Santiago only occasionally for a flying trip to Guantanamo for coal. She was there engaged in coaling, July 1st, when the news came that the fleet would attack Santiago the following day, while General Shafter's army, then supposed to be about to march on the city, conducted an attack by land. The crew was actively engaged in getting coal on board, a dirty job at the best and a fatiguing one as well. Everything indicated that this would be a serious engagement and a decisive one. The Indiana would not be in it unless work was pushed. So all hands proceeded to hustle in obedience to orders. Every man knew why the rush orders were given, and that added tonic to weary limbs. So well did the men work that all the coal was on board at midnight of the first day of July. It was up anchor and away at once with never a minute for rest. The Indiana arrived and joined the rest of the fleet before Santiago early on the morning of July 2d. At daylight, which on this morning was half-past five o'clock, the guns of the ships opened fire, the forts promptly replied, and the engagement was on. For over two hours the firing was incessant,

JUST AFTER THE SAN JUAN DE PUERTO RICO ACTION OF MAY 12, 1898

Paymaster Frazer, Gunner Mallery, Master-At-Arms Keating, and some of the "men behind the guns."

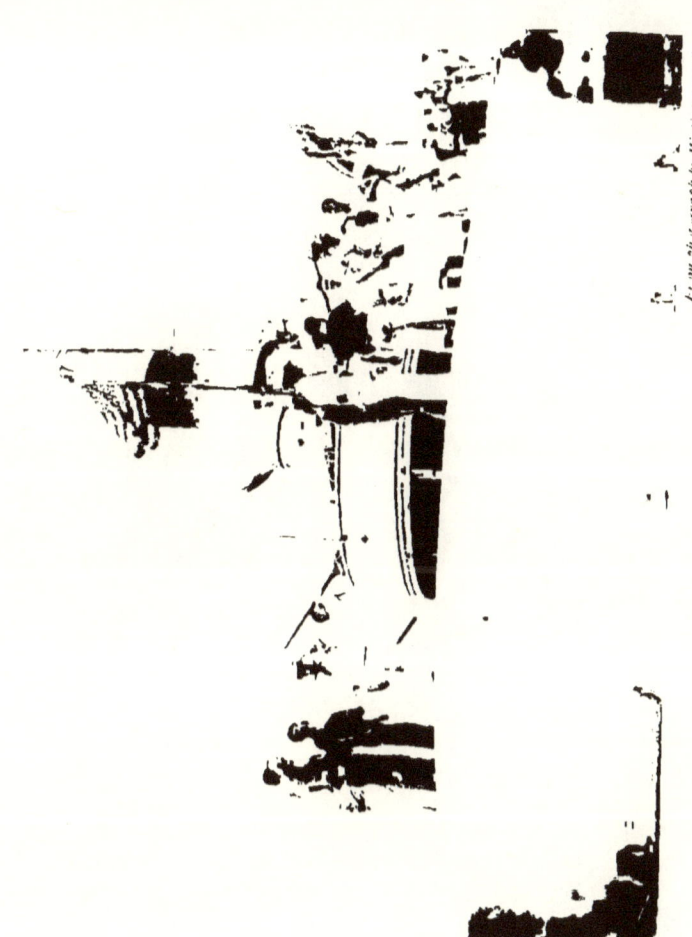

"AS THE CREW GATHERED ON THE TOP OF THE TURRETS."
From photograph by H. G. Casad.
(During bombardment of July 2d)

and only when every Spanish gun was silenced the bombardment ceased. The Indiana escaped injury, not being hit a single time by any of the many shells falling and exploding all around her.

The *Squadron Official Bulletin*, published during the Santiago blockade on the New York, gives the credit for shooting away the Spanish flag on the Morro to either the Indiana or the Oregon, and the Indiana's people feel sure one of their guns did that bit of work.

RANGE INDICATOR

Used in action to show distance of ship from the enemy

CHAPTER III

MEMORABLE JULY THIRD

The Part taken by the Indiana in the Exciting and Historical Events of that Day at Santiago. Her Eager Pursuit of a Supposed Spanish Battleship. The Sad Work of Mercy following the Battle. Official Orders of Congratulation. The Victorious Return North.

AFTER the bombardment came the great event of July 3d, which resulted in the destruction of an entire fleet of the enemy's ships of war (with the exception of one which remained afloat a day longer). Here the Indiana played a very important part. The official reports and records tell the story. They tell that the Indiana was closest in to the fleeing ships as they emerged one by one from the mouth of Santiago Harbor, that she gave and took the first fire of nearly every one of the Spanish vessels. In a report made by Commander J. G. Eaton, commanding the Resolute, which vessel was very close by during the early part of the fight, to Admiral Sampson, and which is on file at the Navy Department, it is stated by that officer that the Indiana stood the brunt of the first part of the fight. An extract from the commander's report is given at the end of this chapter.

"July 3, 1898," will always remain a marked date in the mental calendar of every navy man who served on board the Indiana, or on any of the other ships that participated in the destruction of Spain's fine fleet of war vessels commanded by Admiral Cervera. The story of that day has been told and retold hundreds of times since its facts were incorporated into the naval history of the world, but it is always of interest to participants as well as those not so actively concerned. Following is a description, written by Chaplain William G. Cassard of the Indiana, of the events of the battle of that day. This story was sent to the Governor of the State of Indiana, with the approval of the Captain of the ship and the Commander-in-Chief of the fleet and the Secretary of the Navy. The correspondence and the article are given in full:

U. S. S. INDIANA, *First Rate*,
GUANTANAMO, CUBA, *July* 20, 1898.

To His Excellency the Governor of Indiana.

Sir: I inclose a description of the part taken by the battleship Indiana in the action of July 3d, between this fleet under Admiral Sampson, and the Spanish fleet, under Admiral Cervera, written by Chaplain Cassard, U.S.N., serving on board the Indiana.

It is my wish, which is shared by all the officers and crew of the Indiana, that your Excellency should hear from us some account of this important service of our ship, which, having been named for your great commonwealth, has always received from the people of Indiana such friendly notice, as well as the most substantial generosity in the gift of the silver service presented to our ship by the State of Indiana.

Your Excellency may be interested to know that in a skirmish with the batteries on the day following the action with Cervera's fleet—that is, on the night of July 4th—a fragment of a shell, which exploded after penetrating the ship, struck one of the chests containing the silver, and bent in the side of the punch bowl, the fragment remaining in the indentation made.

The question had been discussed as to placing the silver on shore when the war began, but it was decided that it would probably be more pleasing to the people of your State, that their gift should share in all the hazards which the ship might undergo.

I have the honor to be, sir, yours very respectfully,

H. C. TAYLOR,
Captain U. S. Navy, Commanding U. S. S. Indiana.

U. S. FLAGSHIP NEW YORK, *First Rate*,
GUANTANAMO BAY, *July* 24, 1898.

To His Excellency the Governor of Indiana.

Sir: I have the honor and pleasure to forward herewith an account of the action of the 3d of July, in which the Indiana took so honorable a part. She upheld then, as she has always done in every respect, the good name of her namesake. Yours very truly,

W. T. SAMPSON,
Rear-Admiral U. S. N., Commander-in-Chief U. S. Naval Force, North Atlantic Squadron.

NAVY DEPARTMENT,
WASHINGTON, *August* 9, 1898.

Sir: It gives me great pleasure to forward you herewith a letter from Rear-Admiral Sampson, Commander-in-Chief United States naval force on the North Atlantic Station, inclosing a letter from Capt. H. C. Taylor, commanding officer of the Indiana, and an account of the part taken by the battleship Indiana in the engagement of July 3d, off Santiago. Very respectfully,

JOHN D. LONG,
Secretary of the Navy.

THE HONORABLE THE GOVERNOR OF THE STATE OF INDIANA,
Indianapolis, Ind.

STORY OF THE SHIP'S ACTION

On the morning of the memorable 3d of July the Indiana lay about two miles off the entrance to Santiago Harbor. The day opened clear and warm, and gave every promise of being not unlike the days of waiting that had preceded it. The hope that Cervera would come out and give battle, or attempt to escape, had been almost abandoned. But there had been no relaxation of vigilance. Searchlights played upon the entrance at night, and a constant and careful lookout was maintained by day; every department of the ship was kept in the highest state of efficiency. This vigilance was to have its reward, beyond our highest expectation, and the matured plans of Admiral Sampson, perfected to the highest point during the many weeks of watching, were to have a triumphant fulfilment. At 9.30 A.M. we went to ordinary quarters. This was to be followed by general muster, and this in turn by church service. The crew was in mustering white, and the officers had donned their best uniforms for the first time in many moons. In fact, we were preparing, in an orderly manner, to carry out the fixed routine of the first Sunday of the month. But it had been ordered otherwise. A page of history was to be made.

This hour was to be henceforth memorable in the story of American triumph and progress. A mighty blow was to be struck for freedom and justice. This southern coast of Cuba is soon to be the theatre of the greatest naval battle in all history. Half of the actors are on the scene, and the others will not keep us long in waiting.

THE LIBRARY OF CONGRESS

Fold-out Placeholder

This fold-out is being digitized, and will be inserted at a future date.

The Indiana left Hampton Roads on January 14th. For nearly six months we had been in Southern waters and under a tropical sun. Through all the long, weary weeks of waiting we had kept the vigils of war. Trying times were these. But some of the excitement of battle and the glory of victory are to be ours. At 9.35 A.M. the lookout in the top sighted smoke rising from the channel and appearing over Morro. This could have but one meaning. The electric word is passed, "Enemy is attempting to escape!" It is now fully realized that the business for which battleships are built is to be transacted. How the scene changes!

A moment since, carrying out the Sunday routine; now the alarm gongs for "general quarters" sound in every part of the ship. Men spring to their places. No time to change clothing, and we go to battle in our best. Are we excited? No; there is haste, but with it is precision. Grim determination is on every face. No mistakes, characteristic of excitement, are made. No accidents occur. Captain Taylor should be, and is, proud of his men, and satisfied with the discipline which prevails in this supreme hour. Almost instantly the black bow of the Maria Teresa, Admiral Cervera's flagship, is seen poking out at the entrance. She is firing her guns as she comes. We are right in range, and her shells go whistling overhead, or fall in the water alongside. How they managed not to hit us will always be a wonder. Her gunners must have been excited and nervous. This, or their gunnery practice does not produce results that would be satisfactory to an American commander.

Now the Indiana's guns begin to thunder their reply. Our range begins at about four thousand yards, and is soon reduced to about twenty-five hundred yards, as we crowd on all speed, closing in on the enemy, according to Admiral Sampson's instructions, impressed upon his captains through the long period of waiting, in wise preparation for just such a moment as this. We use every gun of our starboard battery, from the great 13-inch to the little one-pounders in the top. One by one the Spanish ships came out, the Teresa being followed by the Vizcaya, the Colon, the Oquendo, the destroyers Furor and Pluton in the order named. Soon all are heading in column to the westward, keeping close inshore. It is to be a running fight. Our ships were disposed about the entrance from west to east in the following order: Brooklyn, Texas, Iowa, Oregon, Indiana, and Gloucester; and in this order they entered into this running engagement, the flagship New York being too far to the eastward to participate in the early part of the engagement. Each of these ships, let it be said, took a creditable and important part in the battle. There is little doubt that every American vessel at some time during the engagement fired at each of the Spanish ships. The fire from our ship (as from all) was indescribably terrific, rapid, and constantly maintained. It is little wonder that the Spaniards were so soon demoralized. To have been on the Indiana as her batteries discharged broadside after broadside of death-dealing projectiles is to understand in some faint degree the speedy and complete destruction of Spain's proud Cape Verde fleet.

At this point, and until all of our ships were well out of range, the shore batteries were firing as they had never fired before. Our ships paid not the slightest heed to them, and only afterward did we remember that they had participated in the engagement. The business of the American ships was to destroy Cervera's squadron. For this had they patiently waited, and now that the opportunity has arrived, no earthly power can turn them aside from this one purpose. Our signal book shows that the only signal made during the entire engagement was that made at the very beginning, "Enemy is attempting to escape." The Commander-in-Chief, coming up in his flagship from the eastward at full speed, saw plainly that none other was needed. Every commanding officer knew what was to be done, and signals would have been superfluous. It soon became apparent that each ship had a certain part to perform in this swiftly moving drama of war. The position of the Indiana with reference to the enemy's ships was such that it seemed wise for us to address ourselves to the Teresa, Oquendo, and the two destroyers. Captain Taylor, therefore, ordered from time to time that our fire should be concentrated upon these vessels in turn. The little Gloucester, under Lieutenant-Commander Wainwright, was aggressively engaging both of the destroyers. We felt that the problem would

"IT WAS DURING A LULL AT THE CLOSE OF THE BATTLE"
(Santiago, July 3, 1898)

be simplified with the destroyers destroyed, so our secondary battery was turned for a time exclusively upon them. One of our 13-inch shells was also fired at the Pluton and struck her amidships, cutting her almost completely in half. She headed for the shore, burning fiercely and with explosions occurring in her compartments at close intervals.

The combined fire of the Indiana and Gloucester now falling upon the Furor, she was sunk before being able to reach shore, very few of her crew escaping. Our fire upon the Teresa and Oquendo had experienced no cessation during the little diversion with the destroyers, but had been kept up from the great guns remorselessly.

Early in the fight a great shout went up from the Indiana as one of our 13-inch shells was seen to strike the port quarter of the Teresa. That this shell exploded was evident from the jets of flame which immediately sprang from every port. The fire thus started in Admiral Cervera's cabin did not cease to burn until the last vestige of woodwork had been destroyed and the iron ribs of his ship left naked and distorted. In an incredibly short space of time it was seen that the Teresa and Oquendo must share the fate of the destroyers. They were both on fire, and their guns almost silenced. As we watched them, they were seen to head inshore, and the white flag was run up on each ship. The Teresa struck first, and then the Oquendo went ashore not more than a half-mile west of the flagship.

There they lay, torn and beaten, a prey to the fast-devouring flames. As we passed these ships in hot pursuit of the Vizcaya, we saw their crews crowding the forecastles and making frantic efforts to get ashore. Some, from the Teresa, were dropping into a solitary boat, while others were throwing themselves bodily into the sea and swimming for life. As they reached the shore they started up the mountain side, as though in dread of the explosions from their own ships. Their fears were not groundless, as terrific explosions, which could only have been caused by the magazines, were seen to occur from time to time. Our natural impulse was to go to the relief of these beaten and miserable creatures, but the stern necessities of war demanded that we keep on our way until the last enemy had been defeated. The Vizcaya gave a slightly better chase than either the Teresa or Oquendo, but in a very short time after the destruction of her sisters, she, too, gave up the fight and headed for the shore. With great masses of flame wrapping the entire afterpart of the ship in a winding sheet of fire, the spectacle was at once grand and terrible. A "sad but glorious" end for a man-o'-war.

When the Indiana got close to the Vizcaya we found that she had received the attention of other ships of our squadron besides the Indiana and had suffered accordingly. It is but simple truth that there was nothing more needed to complete the defeat and destruction of the Spanish cruiser. The great victory is almost complete—only the Cristobal Colon is still afloat—and just one hour and forty minutes have elapsed since the enemy was reported to be "attempting" to escape. "Attempting"—yes, the word was not used without discrimination.

For some time now the Indiana had been giving her attention to the Teresa, Oquendo, and the destroyers, while the Brooklyn, Texas, and Oregon had been hastening to the westward in pursuit of the Colon, which they finally overtook and captured at 1.50 P.M. The New York coming up from the eastward at this juncture, and seeing the battle practically over, signalled the Indiana to return and guard the entrance to Santiago, now left without any protection.

Now when it appeared that our fighting was over for the day, Captain Taylor made a speech of characteristic modesty and brevity to the men, gathered without prearrangement on the forecastle: "I want to congratulate you upon your good work. We have had a great part in putting the enemy on the beach. No ship has done more." A mighty shout of victory, and then three hearty cheers and a tiger for Captain Taylor. The Captain had not left the bridge during the engagement, and was covered with the grimy, slippery, indescribable saltpetre deposit, so well known on men-o'-war.*

---

* It was during the lull at the close of the battle, after all the Spanish ships had been beached, that the Gloucester came alongside and Lieutenant-Commander Wainwright megaphoned word across to Captain Taylor on the Indiana's bridge that he had orders to put a number of Spanish prisoners on board the Indiana, including Admiral Cervera. When the men of the

Our way now diverges sharply from that of the ships left in pursuit of the Colon, and for the remainder of the day we have a history all our own. Carrying out the orders just received from the Commander-in-Chief, we swung around and headed back for the old berth off Morro. We had barely arrived at our accustomed station when the Resolute, coming from the eastward, reported a large Spanish battleship off Guantanamo and heading to the westward. This information had been signalled by the army from shore. The transports, which had been well to the eastward during the action, were now seen approaching us under all possible steam. The coming of the Spaniard had been reported to them, and they were in wild flight. We could not see just what Spanish battleship could be in these waters, but as the information seemed to be authentic, we prepared to meet the enemy. A large battleship was just the kind of game we were gunning for that day, and the Captain at once decided to meet the Spaniard half-way. We started eastward full speed ahead, and soon had the satisfaction of sighting the stranger.

The rapidly approaching ship showed up large, white, and positively a battleship. This much was clear, and there seemed to be little doubt that the colors were those of Spain. We now fully anticipated a single-handed contest with a foeman worthy of our steel. Our guns were kept trained with care, and but the word was needed to send our shells crashing into the white sides of the supposed Spaniard. But soon we saw a string of international signals run up at the signal yard-arm, and read there the nationality and name of the ship which had caused such consternation among the transports.

---

crew who had swarmed out of the close, hot turrets, and from other battle stations, on to the forecastle heard this, there arose a cheer of exultation at the mention of the Admiral's name. But this was quickly stopped by the Captain, who called down from the bridge:

"Boys, don't cheer. He is a brave man and he has fought well."

The Spanish Admiral did not come on board after all; but if he had, the admonition of the Captain, expressing so very soon after the fight what the whole country conceded afterwards, would have insured him a courteous reception, just as the junior officers and enlisted men of the vanquished fleet received when they were placed on board.

She was an Austrian, and her name was the Maria Theresa. We still kept our guns moving around to starboard, so as to bear on the battleship, as we suspected a possible ruse. The red, white, and red of the Austrian's flag showed up clearly, and it seems just as well at this writing that the white in the flag was not discolored, so as to closely resemble the yellow centre-bar in the flag of Spain. Had such been the case, there might have been international complications. The Austrian Captain sent an officer on board the Indiana on a visit of courtesy. He was conducted to Captain Taylor on the bridge, and was surprised to learn that we had just been in action, astounded when informed of the destruction of the Spanish ships, and well-nigh paralyzed upon finding that we had sustained no casualties. While the ships were lying side by side, the Austrian band was mustered forward and played "Hail, Columbia." This was answered by a cheer from the Indiana, and so an incident was pleasantly closed which at one time bore the sinister aspect of war.

It was now two o'clock in the afternoon, and officers and men partook of a well-earned dinner. We were now heading west, and about an hour later two expeditions were sent ashore in small boats. One of these was military in character and the other was to carry surgical relief to the crews of the Teresa and Oquendo. Lieutenant Decker was in command of the military expedition, and went in to where the Pluton had been run ashore and abandoned.* He went in carefully, with arms lying convenient for use, expecting possible resistance, as the wrecked Pluton was within the Spanish lines about Santiago.

He soon found, however, that the few scattered Spaniards had neither means nor disposition to offer resistance. In abandoning their boat they had been compelled to swim ashore, and most of them were entirely destitute of clothing. Among those found by Mr. Decker was Lieutenant Nouval, an officer from the Furor. In jumping from his boat as it was going down, his leg had been caught in the propeller and cut off below the knee. Seventeen in all were found and brought off to the Indiana, where they were cared for with all possible kindness. It was

---

* Names of boats' crews at end of the eighth chapter.

found necessary to amputate the leg of Lieutenant Nouval at a higher point, as the bone was left jagged and exposed by the original and accidental amputation. The operation was performed by our senior surgeon, Dr. Ferebee, and was borne with great fortitude by the Spanish lieutenant.

The relief party to the Teresa and Oquendo was composed of officers and men who volunteered for this service, the officers being Captain Waller of the Marine Corps, Ensign Olmsted, Dr. Costigan, Cadet Helm, and Chaplain Cassard. Every one in the ship, beginning with the Captain, was anxious that this humane service should be rendered.

The American sailor is always ready for a stand-up fight, and can be relied upon, when so engaged, to conduct himself with bravery and skill, but he has only charity for the fallen foe. It was commonly remarked in all the ships that the men who fought with inspiring enthusiasm until the enemy was defeated, at once rallied with equal interest to the work of succoring the prisoners as they came aboard our ships. So it came about that our relief expedition left the ship with the hearty good-will and best wishes of all on board.

Upon arriving on shore a sad spectacle met our gaze. On either hand lay the burning ships Teresa and Oquendo. Explosions on board were frequent, and the guns which had been left loaded by the escaping crews were being discharged by the heat. The Spanish prisoners on shore and the Americans who were relieving them were in constant and great danger from these sources, and that no casualties were thus caused is a matter of real wonder. However, the work of relief went forward without any attention being paid to this danger. No precautions could be taken against it, and so it was simply disregarded.

We found about six hundred prisoners from the two ships gathered at a common point near the Teresa, where the best landing could be had. The Harvard was lying just outside of the wrecks, and her boats were carrying off the uninjured prisoners. Little had been done for the wounded, of whom there were about forty, owing to the absence of physicians and medical stores.

We saw only three dead on the beach, and these were drowned in an attempt to get ashore from the burning ships. Those who had been killed in action had been left where they fell, and there is little doubt that many of the wounded shared a similar fate. With the ships burning so fiercely when abandoned, and every crack and crevice permeated with the blinding, suffocating smoke of battle, the wonder is, not that so many were lost, but that so large a number escaped. We began without delay to care for the wounded. Many of them were lying in the sand, their wounds simply covered with rags. Dr. Costigan went to work with a will, the rest of us lending such assistance as, in the inexperience of laymen, we were able.

One Spanish surgeon had escaped, but so shattered in mind and nerve and body by the awful experiences of the day as to be of little assistance. However, he obeyed the instructions of our surgeon with a spirit which won our highest admiration.

All of the prisoners were parched with thirst, and we were greeted with profoundest thanks, as with cup and canteen we went about doling out the warm water, of which, fortunately, we had carried a good supply. It was eight o'clock before the last prisoner, including the wounded, had been sent off to the Harvard. A large bonfire had been built, and this threw its light upon the actors in this closing scene of the day which had been fraught with such different meaning to the countries at war. In the sombre-shadowed background stood a group of Cuban soldiers. Is not this scene typical of the whole drama of the war? Here are the two contending parties, and here also the Cubans, whose war for freedom had precipitated this larger war.

Upon returning to the Indiana, we found that the care of over two hundred prisoners had fallen to our lot at least for the night, and everything possible was done to make them comfortable. Many of these prisoners were totally destitute of clothing, and the man who had a suit of pajamas was the envy of his companions. It was, therefore, necessary to clothe most of them, and it was noticeable that they donned the uniform of Uncle Sam with calm philosophy and without a protest. Among our prisoners were seven officers, and these were entertained in the wardroom and clothed largely from the private wardrobes of our officers. They were modest and gentlemanly in deportment, and seemed deeply touched by the consideration shown them.

From Photograph by Chaplain Cassard, July 4, 1898.

SPANISH PRISONERS ON BOARD THE INDIANA

"It was noticeable that they donned the uniform of Uncle Sam with calm philosophy and without a word of protest."

After the most exciting day that many of us had ever known, we were not to have a night of rest. The care of this large number of prisoners kept many awake. The wounded required treatment and nursing. It was far in the morning of July 4th before the spirit of repose came upon our ship, and then we fell to dreaming of the battle, of the wounded, of the dead—of war.

The officers and men of Cervera's squadron did a heroic thing when they came out of Santiago Harbor. The captain of one of the torpedo-boat destroyers told us that he had scarcely slept for more than a month, having made nightly trips of observation to the entrance, in hopes of finding opportunity for the fleet to get out, but always finding the tireless searchlight playing full on the entrance, and had gone back disappointed to his admiral. No more chivalric was the charge of the Light Brigade, no more certain of death were the men who composed it than were many of those who sailed with Cervera. Let Americans rejoice in the victory of our ships, but let them respect the bravery of their fallen foe.*

On the morning of July 14th our entire ship's company was mustered on the quarter-deck, and the following orders were read:

NORTH ATLANTIC STATION,
U. S. FLAGSHIP NEW YORK, *First Rate*,
GUANTANAMO BAY, CUBA, *July* 8, 1898.

Squadron General Order No. 12:

The following despatches were received from the President of the United States and the Secretary of the Navy, and are

---

* Immediately after the destruction of the fleet the following telegram was sent by the Commander-in-Chief to the Navy Department at Washington:

"The fleet under my command offers the nation as a Fourth of July present the destruction of the whole of Cervera's fleet. Not one escaped. It attempted to escape at 9.30 this morning; at two, the last ship, the Cristobal Colon, had run ashore sixty miles west of Santiago, and hauled down her colors. The Infanta Maria Teresa, Oquendo, and Vizcaya were forced ashore, burned and blown up within twenty miles of the port. Loss— one killed and two wounded. Enemy's loss probably several hundred from gun-fire, explosions, and drowning. About 1,300 prisoners, including Admiral Cervera. The man killed was George H. Ellis, chief yeoman of the Brooklyn."

published for the information of the officers and men of this command.

WILLIAM T. SAMPSON,
*Rear-Admiral, Commander-in-Chief U. S.
Naval Force, North Atlantic Station.*

EXECUTIVE MANSION,
WASHINGTON, D. C., *July* 4, 1898.

You have the gratitude and congratulation of the whole American people. Convey to noble officers and crews, through whose valor new honors have been added to the American Navy, the grateful thanks and appreciation of the nation.

WILLIAM MCKINLEY.

NAVY DEPARTMENT,
WASHINGTON, *July* 4, 1898.

The Secretary of the Navy sends you and every officer and man of your fleet, remembering equally your dead comrade, grateful acknowledgment of your heroism and skill. All honor to the brave. You have maintained the glory of the American Navy.

JOHN D. LONG.

U. S. S. INDIANA, *First Rate*,
OFF SANTIAGO DE CUBA, *July* 9, 1898.

Order :

The commanding officer congratulates the officers and crew of the Indiana upon the excellent work performed lately by the ship. The laborious coaling at Guantanamo, not ending until nearly midnight, was followed by the ship's immediate departure for Santiago, and upon our arrival there, by daylight on July 2d, we were ordered at once into a general action with the batteries. This proved to be a close action, and the effectiveness of our fire was commented upon by all who saw it, and was more creditable, since all hands went into action with the fatigue and dirt of coaling still upon them. The following day, without any warning, the Spanish squadron came out, and found us ready and eager to engage them. In the battle which followed, the coolness, bravery, and patriotism of officers and crew were displayed in the highest degree. The commanding officer congratulates all persons on board upon their useful and honorable services in this great victory, and the complete destruction of the enemy's squadron.

H. C. TAYLOR,
Captain U. S. Navy, Commanding.

The officers and men of the battleship Indiana join in greeting to the Chief Executive and citizens, not forgetting the noble

ANOTHER VIEW OF THE SPANISH PRISONERS ON BOARD THE INDIANA

women of the great State of Indiana. It is indeed a proud honor and an exalted privilege to be permitted to serve one's country in so mighty a ship, named for so grand a commonwealth.

EXECUTIVE DEPARTMENT, STATE OF INDIANA,
INDIANAPOLIS, IND., *August* 13, 1898.

Sir: I have the honor of acknowledging the receipt of your valued communication of July 20th, under date of Guantanamo, Cuba, with enclosed account of the part taken by the battleship Indiana in the now celebrated naval engagement of July 3d, off Santiago de Cuba, as graphically described by Chaplain Cassard.

To say that I am profoundly grateful for your kind thoughtfulness in this matter but poorly expresses the deep sense of feeling entertained by the people of this State and myself for the generous courtesy you have manifested in thus supplying an authentic and thrilling recital of the brilliant operations of the great battleship, under the direction of officers who have proved themselves worthy of the applause and admiration, not only of the United States, but of the civilized nations of the earth.

The people of our State are justly proud of the invincible battleship that bears the honored name of this great commonwealth, and they are equally proud of the victorious officers and crew who have so successfully coöperated in giving this vessel one of the foremost places in the history of the navies of the world.

Again thanking you in the name of the people of Indiana for your kind and thoughtful consideration, I have the honor to be,

Yours respectfully,

JAMES A. MOUNT,
Governor.

CAPTAIN H. C. TAYLOR, U. S. S. INDIANA.

REPORT OF THE EXECUTIVE OFFICER TO THE COMMANDING OFFICER OF THE ENGAGEMENT WITH CERVERA'S FLEET

U. S. S. INDIANA, *First Rate*,
OFF SANTIAGO DE CUBA, *July* 5, 1898.

Sir: 1. In accordance with paragraph 525, U. S. Navy Regulations, I have the honor to submit the following report relative to the engagement with the Spanish squadron off Santiago de Cuba on the morning of the 3d instant.

2. The behavior of the officers and crew while under fire was, in my opinion, excellent. The division officers deserve great credit for the rapid and effective fire which was maintained

during the action. The guns worked well and the supply of ammunition was sufficient. The divisions were commanded as follows: Lieutenant R. Henderson, powder division; Lieutenant Roy C. Smith, first division (forward 13-inch turret); Lieutenant F. L. Chapin, fourth division (after 13-inch turret); Lieutenant B. C. Decker, second division; Lieutenant Thomas Washington, third division. No. 3 turret (starboard forward 8-inch) was commanded by Ensign P. N. Olmsted. The 6-pounders were commanded by Captain L. W. T. Waller, U.S.M.C.

3. The ship was struck only once, by a fragment of a shell or a projectile of very small calibre, as the marks were very slight, and no damage was done to the ship, except the wrecking of the gig by the blasts of our own guns.

4. I observed great advantage in the use of smokeless powder for the secondary battery, and would recommend a new supply be obtained as soon as possible as the amount on hand is very small.

Very respectfully,

JOHN A. RODGERS,
Lt.-Comdr. and Executive Officer.

THE COMMANDING OFFICER, U. S. S. INDIANA.

NOTE.—The Executive Officer has special charge, under the Commanding Officer, of the battery of a man-of-war in action. His personal coolness and ability are very essential factors in battle, as was fully demonstrated in the case of the Indiana in her various engagements.

EXTRACT FROM COMMANDER EATON'S REPORT OF HIS OBSERVATION OF THE BATTLE.

U. S. S. RESOLUTE,
NAVY YARD, NEW YORK, *September* 3, 1898.

Sir: I consider it my duty to lay before you the following report of the events witnessed by myself in the action of July 3, 1898, off Santiago.

The Resolute, which I commanded, lay just east of the Indiana, distant from her one thousand feet, and about two and six-tenth miles from the Morro, when the Maria Teresa was sighted.

The Indiana had been near the Morro, but about nine o'clock circled to the eastward with a port helm, leaving the Resolute within the arc of the circle described by the fleet. The Resolute was then turned under a slow bell and stopped when the Indiana was due west of us, and just outside the circle of fighting ships. The Gloucester was to the northward and eastward, nearly off Aguadores.

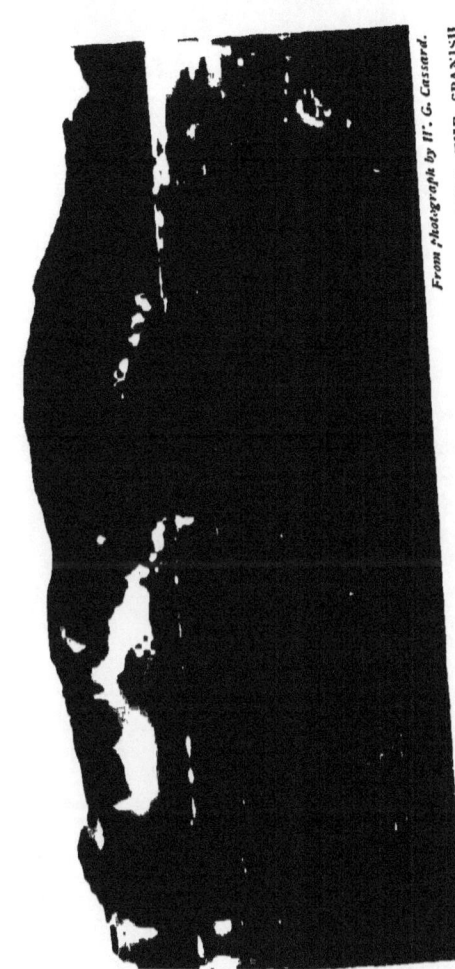

"TWO BURNING, SMOKING WRECKS OF WHAT WERE A LITTLE WHILE BEFORE THE SPANISH SHIPS MARIA TERESA AND OQUENDO."

From photograph by W. G. Cassard.

As the Maria Teresa appeared, the Iowa fired a 6-pounder and hoisted signal. Within a few seconds of this shot (not more than five or ten) all the Spanish batteries opened, and at the same instant the port broadside of the Maria Teresa was discharged. It seemed to me that all or nearly all of these shots and shells were fired at the Indiana, and as the Resolute lay directly in line, the water around the Indiana and the Resolute was alive with the fall of projectiles.

Before the Vizcaya appeared, the Indiana opened with her heavy guns, and, with screws whitening the water astern, was heading for the Morro.

As the Vizcaya came out I distinctly saw one of the Indiana's heavy shells strike her abaft the funnels, and the explosion of this shell was followed by a burst of flame which, for the moment, obscured the afterpart of the Vizcaya.

The Vizcaya fired her port battery apparently at the Indiana, for many of the shells struck about and beyond the Resolute, which was then headed east.

The Cristobal Colon, as soon as she was clear off Morro point, fired her first broadside at the Indiana.

The Oquendo, in coming out, also fired her first broadside at the Indiana, and I could see some of the Indiana's shells strike the Oquendo as she steamed south.

Following close astern on the Colon and the Oquendo came the destroyer Furor, and I distinctly saw her struck by an 8-inch or 13-inch shell from the Indiana, which was followed by an explosion and flames aboard the Furor.

During all this time the Indiana had been steaming ahead and I roughly estimated that she was then about three thousand yards from the Oquendo and the Furor.

From the position of the ships engaged it appeared to me that the Indiana was the first to close with the escaping enemy, and though I could see the Teresa and Vizcaya sweeping across her course, it was apparent that the Indiana's shells were the first to reach them. This was due, first, to the Indiana's proximity; and, second, to the fact that the Indiana had a fair beam target on each ship as it came out.

In addition to the heavier shells noted as striking the enemy, we could count many lighter projectiles from the secondary battery exploding on board, and as the Indiana's fire was incessant, I took these to be from her guns.

The Spanish officers who were prisoners from the Colon and the Vizcaya have since told me that the fire from the Indiana and the Oregon, as they (the Spaniards) passed from the harbor, was deadly in its destructiveness, and that although the Colon escaped with small injury, due to her greater speed, and because in a measure covered by other ships, the Vizcaya was hopelessly crippled before she had gone a mile from the Morro.

I have ventured to address you this letter, as I had exceptional opportunities for observation during this part of the engagement, and it has seemed to me that the very important part taken by the Indiana in the first part of the action should be laid before you.

After the tremendous activities of the 2d and 3d of July, the Indiana and the other battleships had no further active work to do until the city of Santiago de Cuba was bombarded at long range on the 10th and 11th of July. This was the last fighting done by our fleet. A few days later the Indiana went to Guantanamo for further repairs to her boilers. At the same time, preparations were made to accompany the fleet which was then fitting out to go across the ocean and make a demonstration against the Spanish coast. Sea stores were taken on board, and everything was about ready for the long voyage when the orders were countermanded upon the signing of the peace protocol.

The foregoing is in brief the story of one ship's part in the last war. It touches on many points of interest, but it does not tell of the many privations, the peculiar combinations which the ship's cooks presented from time to time for the consumption of hungry sailors, but of which little has been said outside the service, for the reason that the regular enlisted man expects various sorts of privations and inconveniences in time of war, and he does not complain seriously when they come.

In all, the Indiana took part in six important actions during the war, and in that time was struck but once with special damage. This was the time the Socapa Battery shell came down through the quarter-deck, and among other damage inflicted left its imprint on the ship's silver punch bowl, as told in the seventh chapter.

After the engagement of July 3d there was a general overhauling and comparison of " souvenirs " gathered after the battle and during the time spent on shore. In the visits to the wrecks of the two ships in whose destruction the Indiana was most concerned, during the days immediately following, quite a collection of " curios " were accumulated and brought on board,

From a photograph by Chaplain Jones.

A VIEW OF THE MARIA TERESA'S QUARTER-DECK AFTER THE BATTLE.

to be later brought north and distributed throughout the country by the officers and enlisted men among friends ashore. Among the articles later exhibited on board the Indiana to many thousands of visitors were a Nordenfeldt machine-gun and a boat anchor from the Maria Teresa, a dingy from the Pluton, and a collection of range-finders, torpedo directors, and firing-pins from the several Spanish ships. Individuals had all sorts of small articles of little value in money, but of much worth for their associations. Pieces of Spanish money, and molten gold and silver which had once been money, were quite numerous on board for a time after the fight.

One of the flags flown during the war and the machine gun were carefully preserved, to be presented to the State whose name the ship bears with appropriate ceremony at the State House in Indianapolis. A section of the steel battle hatch through which a section of the shell that entered the quarter-deck penetrated has been presented to the University Club of New York properly inscribed.

CHAPTER IV

EXTRACTS FROM THE LOG OF THE INDIANA

May 4th, 5th, and 11th (cruising from Havana to San Juan); May 12th (San Juan de Puerto Rico); June 22d (Santiago Forts); July 2d (Santiago Forts); July 3d (Cervera's Fleet); July 4th and 5th (Mercedes Affair); July 10th (Bombardment Santiago); July 11th (Bombardment Santiago).

THE following extracts from the ship's log of the Indiana add, in many ways, details which are omitted in the story of the war as told in the remainder of this book. It tells the story as the officers of the deck saw it from day to day as history was being made. The extracts begin on May 4th, when the Indiana sailed from the blockading station off Havana with the squadron in search of Admiral Cervera's fleet, then on its way from Spain.

WEDNESDAY, MAY 4, 1898

Record of the Miscellaneous Events of the Day

8 P.M. to Midnight.—Clear and pleasant. Gentle and moderate breezes from E. N. E. and east. Moonlight; first hour lying to. About 8.50 Iowa had taken Terror in tow and started ahead. . . . The squadron got under way about 9.10, the Montgomery astern of flagship and the Detroit astern of this ship; the Niagara between the two.

THURSDAY, MAY 5, 1898

[Cruising with squadron.]
8 A.M. to Meridian.—Clear and pleasant. . . . At 9.30 mustered at quarters. Then went to general quarters; ready in six minutes, secured in six minutes. Had instruction at battery. Withdrew charges and shell from guns of No. 3 turret for adjustment of sights; then reloaded. Gunner Mallery inspected maga-

zinc flood cocks, drains, and sea valves; found them in good
condition. At 9 slowed and stopped, the flagship and other
vessels having done so. Flag took Terror in tow. At 9.30 went
ahead again. Following in wake of Iowa during watch. At
9.40 valve-stem of low-pressure cylinder of starboard main engine broke. From that time went ahead with port engine, making use of about 20° starboard helm to keep course, and making
about 5 knots. . . . At 8.10 sighted barque on starboard hand.
As she came abeam, about 9, flagship hoisted colors, fleet doing
so also. Barque hoisted Spanish colors at mizzen. New York
signal to Montgomery, whereupon the latter headed for barque,
cast off tow-line of Porter, and at 9.01 fired gun "heave-to" the barque. At 9.09 Montgomery sent boat to barque.
At same time flag signalled Porter to come within hail; then
sent her to barque and Montgomery. At 9.17 Spanish barque
dipped colors three times. About 10 A.M. "M" signalled
"F," "Vessel Spanish, from Argentine Confederation bound
Havana, Cuba. Cargo beef." * As fleet went ahead Porter went
with "F," leaving Montgomery with barque. At end of watch
Montgomery coming up astern. Hauled down colors at 10.30.

Meridian to 4 P.M.—Clear and pleasant. Gentle breezes from
east. Steaming with all boilers, port engine, in wake of squadron. . . . Squadron smoke in sight ahead until near end of
watch, when lost it. Montgomery coming up astern. A brigantine passed to starboard, and at 1.30, when bearing about W. by
S. from us, distant three miles, intercepted by Montgomery,
which fired two shots across her bow, heaving her to. She was
eventually taken in tow by the Montgomery, which resumed
course to eastward.* When in signal distance prize appeared to
show American colors over Spanish. Press yacht Anita passing
to the eastward about one o'clock was hailed and asked if she
intended stopping anywhere to eastward. She replied yes, at
Cape Haiti for coal, and when asked if she would take Lieutenant Whitney of the Army as passenger, consented. Lieutenant
Whitney was therefore put aboard about 1.40. . . . At 3.40
made strange vessel to S. E., steamer with two masts. Montgomery and prize heading for her at end of watch. . . .

4 to 8 P.M.—Generally clear and pleasant. Gentle breeze
from east. About 4.05 started in chase of steamer inshore.
Made signal to Montgomery to give chase. Went to quarters
for muster at 4.10. Made out steamer to be the revenue cutter
Hamilton. Returned to cruise at 4.25. . . . Land sighted
about along starboard beam. The Montgomery passed this ship
about 6.45. At 7 started starboard engine. At 7.10 stopped

---

* See "Prizes," Chapter VIII.

port engine to replace piston packing. At 7.15 sighted Grande Cay Light on starboard beam. . . .

8 P.M. to Midnight.—Fair and pleasant. Gentle breezes from east. At 9.25 started port engine. At 10.20 Paredon Light bore S. S. W. (abeam) distant 5.7 miles, and at 11 bore W. S. W. At 10.50 sighted Lobos Light bearing E. ¾ S. just in the horizon. . . .

WEDNESDAY, MAY 11, 1898

Meridian to 4 P.M.—Generally clear and warm. Gentle breeze from east. At 1.30 sounded call to general quarters. The Captain inspected the ship. Secured and held general muster. The Captain addressed the crew. . . .

4 to 8 P.M.—Fair and pleasant. Gentle breeze from east. Swell from Nd. and Wd. At 4.30 mustered at quarters. At about 4.50 the squadron stopped and the Commander-in-Chief transferred his flag to the Iowa. During watch made preparations for battle. At end of watch standing in column, Iowa leading. At 7.05 started fires in boiler A. . . .

8 P.M. to Midnight.—Clear and pleasant. Gentle breeze from east. . . . Keeping position in column on Iowa's port quarter. . . .

THURSDAY, MAY 12, 1898

Commences and until 4 A.M.—Clear and pleasant. Bright moonlight, moon rising about 12.10. Gentle breeze from E. N. E. In column steaming about S. S. E. ¾ E. At 1.45 connected up "A" boiler. At 2 stopped ice machine. Lights in sight ahead like the city lights of San Juan. At 3 called all hands clear ship for action. About 3 o'clock slowed to keep position in column, the flag having slowed. About 3.30 took in patent log. At end of watch going ahead slow in column, course S. S. E., making preparations for battle.

4 to 8 A.M.—Fair and pleasant. Light to gentle breeze from E. N. E. At the beginning standing in for San Juan de Puerto Rico in column, natural order, Iowa (flagship) leading, followed by Indiana, New York, Amphitrite, and Terror. Detroit 1,000 yards ahead of Iowa and Wompatuck 500 yards on starboard bow. Montgomery to rear of column and stopping to westward of Cabra Island. At 4.07 went to general quarters and stood slowly for Salinas Point. In wake of Iowa. At this time the lights of the city were plainly visible to the southward and eastward. At daylight, being close inshore, head of column turned to eastward, and at 5.20 Iowa opened on batteries at a range of 4,000

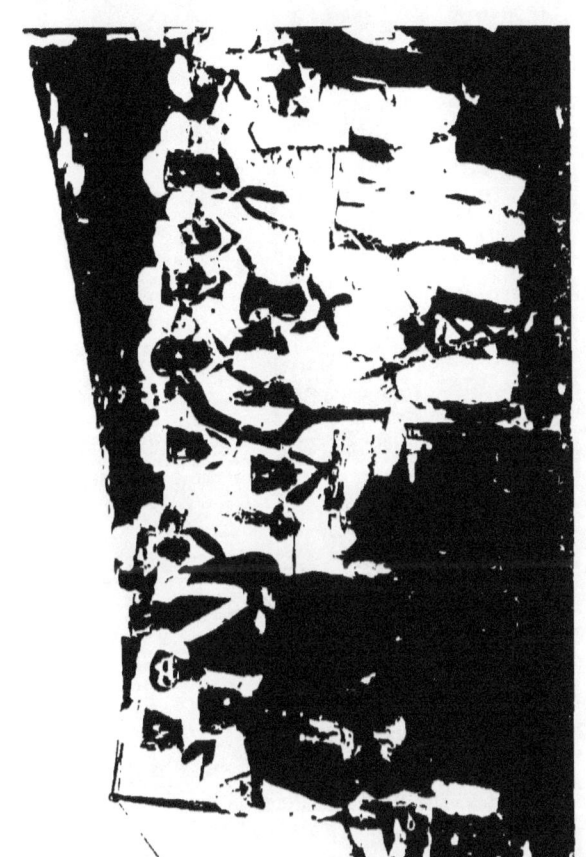

THE BAND

Composed of musically inclined members of the Ship's company, this organization made much pleasure for all hands during the sometimes monotonous hours of inactive war duty.

yards. Indiana began firing at 5.22, and other ships followed in succession as they came in range, and leading ships unmasked the batteries. The fire was not returned by the shore batteries for some time, and, so far as could be seen from the ship, only two shots were fired during first circle. When within about 1,000 yards of the Morro, head of column turned to Nd. and Wd. and squadron continued to circle, as ordered by Commander-in-Chief, making three complete runs over the course. During first run all guns were used; the remainder of the time only large calibres. A number of the enemy's shots went over us, and some fell near us, but the ship was not struck and no injury was done to personnel or material. In preparation for action set adrift first whaleboat, and threw overboard some smaller articles.

8 A.M. to Meridian.—Generally clear. Gentle breeze from Nd. and Ed. At 8 Iowa made signal 61—16—C. The squadron withdrew to the westward. The batteries on shore maintained fire until ships were out of range. At 9.35 the Captain repaired on board Iowa. At 10.45 secured ship. "A" came on our port quarter. Took position on port quarter of "A," and being too close steamed ahead. Received from New York a valve stem to replace one broken in passage to San Juan. At noon, made noon reports by signal. At end of watch, lying to. Smooth sea. Expended the following ammunition during engagement: Ten 13-inch, nineteen 8-inch, twenty-nine 6-inch common shell and full charges; forty-eight common and twenty-two armor-piercing 6-pounder shell, and twenty-two 1-pounder common shell.

WEDNESDAY, JUNE 22, 1898

Commences and until 4 A.M.—Partially cloudy, clearing toward end of watch. Gentle breeze from N. E. Made the following changes of course—at 12.59, 27—C—8, at 1.55, 27—C—22. During first hour took position at head on centre column. Land in sight on port beam. Sighted searchlight of vessel off Cabanas. This light bore abeam about 3.50. At end of watch steaming course N. E. by E., speed eight knots. Made signals during watch as per signal record book. Steam, 80. Revolutions, starboard, 56.4; port, 56.6.

4 to 8 A.M.—Fair and warm. Light breezes from N. E. Standing in heading convoy for Daiquiri. Cleared ship for action and went to general quarters about 5.35. At 6.50 transports and boats being ready for disembarking off Daiquiri, made signal to St. Louis to act at discretion as this vessel was ordered to Santiago; then stood on for station off Santiago. Upon ap-

proaching Daiquiri the Spanish flag was hauled down from one of the blockhouses, and the cars and houses near the town were set on fire. At 7 secured the battery. At end of watch standing W. ½ N. to join the squadron off Santiago.

8 A.M. to Meridian.—Fair to clear, hazy. Gentle breeze between N. E. and S. E. Texas opened fire at 8.10 from position about four thousand yards to S. W. of Morro. Gloucester and Eagle opened later off Aguadores, and Annapolis and Helena off Altares. Troops apparently landing at Daiquiri. At 8.25 stopped with New York to southward and Morro bearing about N. W. At 9.25 received signal to go close inshore. Went to general quarters. Opened fire slowly when five thousand to six thousand yards from battery to east of Morro. Fired also at battery on crest of hill to west of entrance. Several shot from this latter battery passed very near ship. Ceased firing and retired at 11.10 in obedience to signal from Brooklyn, New York having passed to eastward out of signal distance. Expended following rounds common shell and full charges: Three 13-inch, ten 8-inch, eleven 6-inch, twenty-seven 6-pounders. End of watch standing to S. S. E. of Morro, distant three miles, at slow speed.

Meridian to 4 P.M.—Fair and warm. Light breezes from S. S. E. Keeping position to eastward of Oregon. First part, auxiliary yachts Gloucester and Eagle shelled blockhouse on shore. Debarkation of troops going on at Daiquiri. At end of watch Morro lighthouse bore N. W. ¾ N.

4 to 8 P.M.—Generally clear, warm. Hazy about horizon. Light airs and breezes from S. S. E. About 4.20 the flagship passed on way to her station. Paraded guard in honor of Commander-in-Chief. At 4.30 mustered at quarters. The New Orleans took station to eastward of this ship about 4.30. After sundown took station with " F " and to eastward. Smooth sea. The Dupont steamed to Daiquiri and returned during watch.

8 P.M. to Midnight.—Fair and warm. Light breezes from S. S. E. shifting to N. Ship drifting throughout watch, occasionally using engines to keep position and bearing of Morro about N. W. ½ W. About 10.45 five guns were fired from the fort. Searchlight from one of the vessels of the squadron turned on entrance to harbor during watch.

SATURDAY, JULY 2, 1898

Commences and until 4 A.M.—Fair and pleasant. Light breezes from N. W. At 2.18 changed course to W. N. W. ¼ W., patent log reading 22.7. Passed a number of transports off

THE LANDING OF TROOPS AT DAIQUIRI
The New Orleans in the centre of the scene
From photograph taken by W. G. Cassard.

Daiquiri and Siboney. At end of watch standing toward Morro Castle to communicate with the flagship.

4 to 8 A.M.—Partly cloudy and warm. Light to gentle breezes from north. First hour of watch standing in toward Morro. Exchanged call letter with flagship. At about 4.30 flagship signalled by Ardois, "Take position between ' F ' and ' Y.' We engage the batteries at daylight. Receive Mr. Staunton's call." At about 4.50 A.M. called all hands clear ship for action. Cleared ship and about 5.25 beat to general quarters. At 5.30 " F " hoisted Gen. Sig. No. 18. Made interrogatory and by wigwag from " F." This signal means close up to firing distance. At 5.40 signal from " F " Tel. 4060—6555—1267—8504. At 5.42 " F " signalled, " Open fire." Commenced firing with main and secondary battery, port side, at 5.43; ceased at 5.45-30, and commenced again at 5.45-45, and ceased at 6.16-20. At 6.17 from " F " Gen. Sig. Neg. 1. Used secondary battery about twenty minutes of the time. At 6.31 commenced firing on battery on Punta Gorda. Commenced at 7.05 with starboard battery, and ceased at 7.31-30. Secondary battery engaged part of the time. At various times during the action ceased firing for a few minutes, while other vessels in range. At about 7.35 drew off, returned to station, and at 7.56 secured. At the beginning of the engagement a few shots were fired from the Spanish batteries, but soon ceased, and during the greater part of the engagement no activity was seen at any of the batteries. While the ships were drawing off four shots were fired from the western battery. Ammunition expended: Seventeen 13-inch, fifty-nine 8-inch, fifty-four 6-inch, and four hundred and forty-three 6-pounders.

8 A.M. to Meridian.—Fair and warm. Light breeze from S. and S. E. Drew charges from 13-inch guns. General clearing. Resumed old station inshore of New York. Routine and message signals as per record book.

Meridian to 4 P.M.—Fine weather at sea, but clouded up ashore to Nd., and the wind, a light breeze from E. and S. Ed., shifted suddenly last hour to N. E. becoming moderate. Rain, thunder, and lightning ashore. Drifting near flagship, Morro bearing about N. W. At 1.30 started dynamo again. At 2 flagship signalled to Indiana, " Commanding officer repair on board," in obedience to which the commanding officer went aboard in the gig; Lieutenant Chapin accompanied him. Boat from " F " brought Lieutenant Capehart. At 2.30 Gloucester sent mail aboard, and at 3.30 the Vixen also sent mail.

4 to 8 P.M.—Generally clear and pleasant. Light airs and breezes from north to N. E. At 4.30 mustered at quarters. Loaded all guns of main battery. The flagship made signal,

"Take your former blockading station inside of us." C. A. Goodwin, G. M. 1 c., returned on board from the flagship. Sent out picket launch with Naval Cadet Smith in charge. About 8 sighted large lights on mountains to the Wd. of Santiago near coast, having appearance of signal lights.

8 P.M. to Midnight.—Clear and pleasant. Light breeze from north. On blockade position until 11.30, when steamed over and relieved the Texas supporting the searchlight vessel.

SUNDAY, JULY 3, 1898

Commences and until 4 A.M.—Clear and pleasant. Light breeze from N. by W. and N. N. W. Barometer steady. Bright moonlight. Took station guarding entrance near ship using searchlight, and remained there during watch, keeping port battery manned and guns trained on entrance.

4 to 8 A.M.—Clear to cloudy. Light and gentle breezes from N. N. E. and N. E. Left station off harbor entrance at daylight and resumed blockading station. Assistant Engineer T. C. Dunlap, U.S.N., was detached from this ship and transferred to the Oregon. Picket launch returned and was hoisted in. Fern arrived towing a barge. Message signals as per record book.

8 A.M. to Meridian.—Clear and warm. Light breezes from the Nd. and Wd. Smooth sea, light swell from Sd. and Ed. Mustered and inspected at quarters at 9.30, preparing for general muster. At 9 the flagship New York made Gen. Sig. 162, and stood to the eastward toward Siboney, ordering the Fern, Hist, and another small craft to follow. While at quarters the Iowa fired two signal guns, apparently to attract attention to the Gen. Sig. 250 which she had hoisted, this being signal for "Enemy's ships escaping." A Spanish armored cruiser was seen emerging from the channel leading into the harbor. Went to general quarters on the instant, and a general action began within a very few minutes. The leading Spanish ship, which eventually proved to be the Infanta Maria Teresa, flying the flag of Vice-Admiral Don Pasquale Cervera, was followed by the other vessels of his squadron as follows—viz.: Vizcaya, Cristobal Colon, Almirante Oquendo, armored cruisers, and the torpedo-boat destroyers Furor and Pluton. The vessels present on the blockade of the American fleet were the Brooklyn (flying Commodore Schley's pennant), Oregon, Iowa, Indiana, Texas, and Gloucester. Our squadron headed to the westward, keeping as nearly abreast the Spanish ships as possible, the latter going, all of them, to the westward and well inshore. This vessel fired on all of them as they came out one by one, and con-

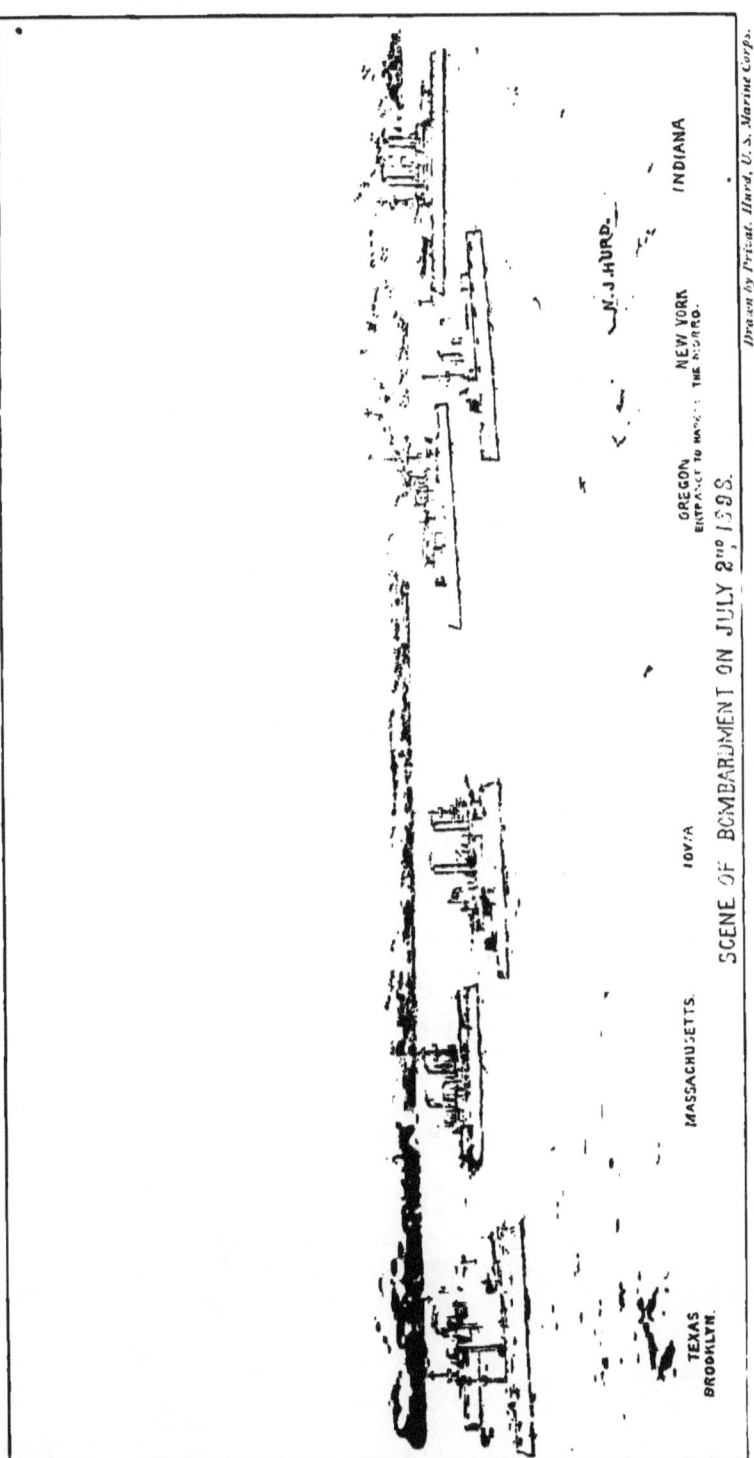

THE INDIANA AND OTHER SHIPS OF THE FLEET FIRING ON THE MORRO AT THE ENTRANCE TO SANTIAGO HARBOR

tinued the action later by firing principally on the Teresa—which had dropped back to third position—Oquendo, Furor, and Pluton. Several shells were seen to take effect on these vessels, particularly on the first and the last two, the two latter being destroyed through the agency of our guns and those of the Gloucester, which vessel engaged them close aboard. Before 10.15 the Maria Teresa and Oquendo were run ashore about five and one-half miles to the westward of the entrance and on fire, and the destroyers were both blown up. Later observed the Vizcaya on fire, and she was run ashore about fifteen miles to the westward of the entrance. The Cristobal Colon at end of watch was well down on western horizon near shore and pursued by the Brooklyn, Texas, and Oregon. Passed the burning vessels Maria Teresa and Oquendo about 11.* At 11.27 the flagship New York came up and passed inshore of this ship, going to the westward at full speed, signalling us Gen. Sig. 2305 and by wigwag, "Go back to entrance of harbor." Returned wigwag signal, "Beg to assist in capture of remaining Spaniard," and at 11.29 made G. S. to her 2877. At 12 were signalled by the Gloucester—Tel. 2823. Then turned and stood to the eastward in obedience to signal. Saw numbers of transports coming westward from Siboney and Daiquiri about noon. At various times observed heavy explosions on board the Oquendo and Maria Teresa, and many men from both vessels on shore, while others were jumping overboard from their bows and others going off in one or two boats. Expended during the action ammunition as follows—viz.: 13-inch common shell and reduced charges, 13 : 8-inch common shell and full charges, 61 ; 6-inch common shell and full charges, 33 ; 6-pounder charges, 1,744 ; 1-pounder charges, 25. No casualties occurred through the enemy's fire, and as far as could be determined only one projectile, apparently a 1-pounder, struck the ship, that being on the side of the after 13-inch turret, making a very slight scar. At end of watch the before-mentioned vessels were in pursuit of the Cristobal Colon, and the New York was going westward at full speed.

Meridian to 4 P.M.—Generally clear and warm. An officer from the Austrian armored cruiser Kaiserin Maria Theresa came on board. Later the ship stood to the westward. The Ericsson came up from the westward to inquire character of vessel which had been reported as an enemy. Two boats were fitted, the steam cutter and third cutter, to aid wounded of ships on shore.

---

* NOTE BY COMMANDING OFFICER.—10.30 was about the time of passing the Maria Teresa and Oquendo, as observed by the Commanding Officer. H. C. TAYLOR, *Captain*.

At end of watch lying-to, Morro bearing about N. by E., the Iowa in sight to westward.

4 to 8 P.M.—Fair and warm. Light breezes and airs from N. N. E. Keeping station off entrance to Santiago Harbor. At 5.10 the Gloucester came near and transferred to us sixty-two prisoners of war. The commanding officer called on board the Iowa. Paraded guard to the Spanish Vice-Admiral Cervera passing in pulling boat to go on board the Iowa. Sent steam cutter and two pulling boats to the assistance of the wounded and captured of the Spanish ships. Message signals as per record book.

8 P.M. to Midnight.—Cloudy to clear. Light breeze from N. Keeping blockading station. Received prisoners and wounded as follows from the Hist: One officer, one hundred and thirty-nine men, of whom five were wounded; from shore by our own boats, one officer from the Furor wounded, fourteen men from the Teresa, one man from the Oquendo, one man from the Furor. Harvard and Brooklyn arrived from westward, the latter bringing news of the capture of the Colon at 1.15, thus accounting for all the Spanish vessels that came out of Santiago this morning.

MONDAY, JULY 4, 1898

Commences and until 4 A.M.—Clear and pleasant. Light to gentle breezes from north and N. N. W. Lying off entrance of harbor of Santiago on blockade. Large number of Spanish prisoners on board. The Dupont passed close aboard, going to the eastward, at 9.45. At 10.25 observed heavy explosion from the Almirante Oquendo, which vessel and the Maria Teresa are still burning. At 10 the Solace joined the blockading force.

4 to 8 A.M.—Generally clear and pleasant. Gentle breeze from N. N. W. The flagship steamed up from the westward about 4.30, standing for Siboney. The English gunboat Alista was sighted to Sd., and a steam launch with an officer was sent to board her. About 7 the steamship Silvia was hove to and boarded, having shown signs of attempting to pass the blockading line. She was boarded and allowed to proceed as she was used by newspaper correspondents. During the watch the Austrian ship Kaiserin Maria Theresa and an English cruiser were sighted to the eastward standing toward the flagship. Later the small English gunboat was seen at the mouth of the harbor. Transferred seven wounded Spanish sailors and one officer to the Solace for treatment. Smooth sea. At daylight dressed ship with national ensign at truck, with flagship.

8 A.M. to Meridian.—Fair and warm. Light airs to moderate breezes from the E. At 9.30 mustered at quarters. Unloaded

THE INDIANA'S BATTLE FLAGS AS THEY FLEW IN THE BREEZE BEFORE SANTIAGO DE CUBA ON THE FOURTH OF JULY, 1898

turret guns. At 11.50 began transferring prisoners to the St. Louis in obedience to signals. At noon fired a salute of twenty-one guns in company with the other ships in honor of the day. At end of watch lying to transferring prisoners. Two British and one Austrian vessel lying to off the entrance to the harbor.

Meridian to 4 P.M.—Clear and warm. Gentle to moderate breezes from E., hauling to S. E. by E. Barometer falling. Drifting and keeping off entrance to harbor. Finished transferring prisoners to St. Louis, having transferred two hundred and nine men and six officers. Two English and one Austrian men-of-war close in near Morro.

4 to 8 P.M.—Cloudy weather; pleasant; stiff breeze from S. E. and E. S. E. Land breeze made last hour from north. At 4.30 mustered at quarters. Loaded 8-inch guns. English and Austrian men-of-war left to the southward and westward. Massachusetts arrived from eastward and was assigned Brooklyn's station. Hoisted in steam launch. Moon rose at 7.45.

8 P.M. to Midnight.—Cloudy and pleasant. Light airs to gentle breezes from the Nd. and Wd. On station to the Sd. and Ed. of Morro. Flagship close inshore. Observed several large fires on mountain and hill-tops to the Nd. and Ed. of Santiago, apparently signal fires. Went to general quarters at 11.30 because of the alarm signal for enemy's ships approaching being given by the Massachusetts and Texas firing at some object inside entrance. East and west shore batteries and mortar battery returned fire. At 11.58 an 8-inch mortar shell struck the ship aft, landing on the flash plate, starboard side, penetrating the main deck, going through the cabin pantry and striking the angle of beam at frame No. 77, where it exploded with great effect, wrecking the battle hatch cover leading down to the after orlop, and making holes in cabin and stateroom bulkheads in vicinity and bending in cabin bulkhead to starboard of fore and aft line.

TUESDAY, JULY 5, 1898

Commences and until 4 A.M.—Generally clear and pleasant. Bright moonlight. Light breeze from north. Secured battery at 12.25. Maintaining station on blockade. At end of watch Morro bearing N. W. Baled water out of Paymaster's storeroom; ran in through fire-hose.

4 to 8 A.M.—Fair and warm. Light variable breezes. Drifting and working engines occasionally to hold blockading station. At end of watch Morro light bore N. W. ½ N. and Aguadores N. ¼ E.

8 A.M. to Meridian.—Clear and warm. Gentle breeze from

S. E. and S. E. by S. Barometer rising slowly. First part of watch, mail to Celtic. At 9.30 went to quarters for muster and exercised at passing the range and infantry. Started fires under boiler F. Frank Rench, F. 1 c., reported expiration of his enlistment. C. M. Rowland, F. 1 c., rating changed to boilermaker.

Meridian to 4 P.M.—Partially clear, pleasant. Gentle to moderate S. E. breezes. Smooth sea. Lying near wrecks of Maria Teresa and Oquendo. Flagship close to them with officers and boats' crews aboard.

4 to 8 P.M.—Generally clear and pleasant. Threatening at times. Light breeze from S. E. shifting to N. E. last hour. At 4.30 mustered at quarters. Lying off the wrecks of the Maria Teresa and the Almirante Oquendo. About 5 started to regain station on blockade. The flagship and the Texas and the Oregon returned to station about 7. Smooth sea; long swell from S. E.

8 P.M. to Midnight.—Fair and pleasant. Light breezes from N. N. E. On blockade station using engines to keep position.

SUNDAY, JULY 10, 1898

Commences and until 4 A.M.—Fair and pleasant. Misty over the land. Light breezes from N. N. W. On blockade, Aguadores bearing N. ¾ W.: at end of watch, Morro not visible.

4 to 8 A.M.—Clear and pleasant. Light to gentle breezes from N. W. by N. Barometer rising. St. Paul arrived from eastward. First part of watch on blockading station, latter part to westward near the Brooklyn.

8 A.M. to Meridian.—Clear and pleasant. Sea breeze made about 9 from E. S. E., increasing to moderate force end of watch. Mustered at quarters at 9.30. J. B. Hedenger, Sea., reported the expiration of his enlistment. Ran over toward Brooklyn and sent boat for mail. Afterward, in obedience to signal, Texas and this ship accompanied Brooklyn to position off Aguadores. Texas stood again to westward, returning at end of watch. Scorpion arrived from eastward. Vesuvius stood to eastward. Transferred John Koehler, App., 2 c., and E. E. Comstock, App., 2 c., to U. S. S. Hornet, sending them to Scorpion for passage. Brooklyn stood to S. E. about 11.30 in chase of steamer flying Norwegian flag and standing to eastward. At 11.45 she fired a blank charge. She was near steamer at end of watch, distant about three miles from this ship.

Meridian to 4 P.M.—Cloudy and pleasant. Moderate breezes from E. by S. Smooth sea. At 2.30 stood to the eastward and later ran in to Siboney Harbor, where put a sick man, A. Paren-

ONE OF THE PENETRATED DECKS, OR HAND PLATES OF THE INDIANA, HIT BY SPANISH SHELL, JULY 4th

teau, Sea., on board the ambulance ship Solace. Received papers, also two men—James Kelley, S. C. 1 c., and T. Jintara, cabin steward—by transfer from the St. Paul. Found the Helena and Machias in the harbor assisting in landing soldiers from several transports recently arrived. Left the harbor at 3.45 in obedience to signal from the Brooklyn to come within hail and stood westward for the Brooklyn.

4 to 8 P.M.—Cloudy and threatening with passing showers. Light breezes from Nd. and Ed. shifting to N. N. W. last hour. Received a message by megaphone from the Brooklyn that that ship would begin a bombardment of the city, firing a gun every two minutes for an hour; that the Texas and then the Indiana would follow. The town bearing north a little west. The Brooklyn began the bombardment at 4.45. Took station astern of the Texas. At 5.10 cleared ship for action; about 5.30 went to general quarters. At 5.30 began firing with stbd. after 8-inch turret. Fired four shots from each stbd. 8-inch turret. The two 13-inch turrets were trained aport. Range nine thousand yards. Ship's position, Morro bearing N. N. W. mag. distant six thousand to seven thousand yards. Fired in direction N. by W. ½ W. to N. by W. ¾ W. Ceased firing after the eight shots and awaited orders. Lying to rest of watch.

8 P.M. to Midnight.—Cloudy and threatening rain. Light breezes and airs from north. At 8.30 took position on blockade, Morro bearing north, distant three miles, in obedience to signal from the Brooklyn. The New York came from the eastward about 10.15 and joined the blockade. Ship drifting on station.

MONDAY, JULY 11, 1898

Commences and until 4 A.M.—Partly cloudy and pleasant. Light airs to breezes from N. N. E. Barometer falling. Using engines to keep blockading station. Morro bearing north.

4 to 8 A.M.—Clear to cloudy. Squall threatening from southward. Light breeze between north and N. E. Keeping blockading station, Morro bearing about north. Tested whistle and siren.

8 A.M. to Meridian.—Generally clear, hot and oppressive. Light airs and breezes from the eastward. At 8.20 took station on blockade three miles south of Morro, in obedience to signal from the Brooklyn at 8.10. At 9.45 observed a tug and lighter moving about in the entrance to harbor beyond Morro. Stood over to the Ed. and Nd. and reported this fact to the flagship New York. At 10 made sick report 9 to flagship. At 10.09 made G. S. 3093. Received a mail from the United States at

10.30 from the Suwanee. At 10.20 made all preparations for bombardment of Santiago with 8-inch guns, the flagship and Brooklyn already having fired a few shots. At 11 began firing with 8-inch guns, the ship lying very close to shore off east end of railway bridge; port battery, 8-inch guns engaged; stream anchor down with wire hawser bent to it. At noon still firing.

Meridian to 4 P.M.—Rainy, with heavy rain and wind squall last hour. Light to moderate breezes from Sd. and Wd. Ceased firing at 12.50, hove up anchor and stood offshore. Expended thirty-seven 8-inch shells. The Yale and Columbia joined the flagship. The Commander-in-Chief visited the Yale. Lying to to the eastward of Aguadores at end of watch.

4 to 8 P.M.—Cloudy, with frequent rain squalls. Light breezes from E. N. E. and east. Drifting during watch. Message signals as per record book. About 7.30 the Vesuvius and Machias joined the flagship and the Brooklyn and Texas stood to the southward.

8 P.M. to Midnight.—Overcast, cloudy, and rainy, with thunder and lightning. Light variable airs to gentle breezes. Barometer unsteady. Drifting throughout watch.

From Photograph by Chaplain Cassard.

A VIEW OF THE DECK BEAMS OF THE MARIA TERESA, AFTER THE FIRE CAUSED BY THE SHELLS OF THE INDIANA AND THE OTHER SHIPS HAD BURNED AWAY ALL THE WOODWORK

CHAPTER V

THE GUN-FIRE

The Indiana's Hail of Death-dealing Metal on Enemy's Forts and Ships. Report of the Ship's Ordnance Officer to the Bureau of Ordnance, of Ammunition expended in the Several Actions of the War.

THIS chapter gives the substantial parts of the report made by the Ordnance Officer of the Indiana, to the Commanding Officer of the ship, and by him sent through official channels to the Bureau of Ordnance, Navy Department, showing the amount of ammunition expended by the battleship in the several actions of the war. This is the record of one ship, but one that poured such a hail of metal on the enemy, both at Santiago and elsewhere, as to cause wonder and astonishment from the spectators and those who have studied the matter since the close of active hostilities.

The report was made in accordance with instructions from the Bureau of Ordnance, requiring a report from each ship of the fleet, which should show not only the amount of ammunition used, but also the rapidity of fire, and how well the guns stood the tests of actual service. Extracts from the report follow:

Engagement with the batteries at San Juan, Puerto Rico, May 12, 1898. Range, 4,000 to 1,400 yards.

The action lasted about two hours and fifty minutes. Smoke interfered considerably, especially during the first countermarch, when the rapid-fire battery was in action, and the fire of the guns was frequently masked by the New York getting on our engaged side. The fire was concentrated principally on the Morro, from which distance was measured by sextant and stadimeter, the height of the light being known. The shooting during the first round was poor, the shots falling short; after that the practice

was excellent, though some of the shots went over and fell in the city. No attempt was made to take intervals between shots. . . .
We have learned from the newspapers and from other sources that a number of our shells failed to explode. Reports as to the damage done are conflicting, but probably was not very great, as the enemy continued to fire nearly all his guns as long as we were in range.

Number of shots fired from each gun or turret and kind of ammunition used:—

13-inch turrets: forward, common shell with full charges 4
13-inch turrets: aft, common shell with full charges 6

Total 13-inch 10

8-inch turrets: starboard, forward, common shell with full charges 8
8-inch turrets: starboard, after, common shell with full charges 10
8-inch turrets: port, after, common shell with full charges 1

Total 8-inch 19

6-inch guns, starboard battery, common shell with full charges 29
6-pounders, starboard battery, armor-piercing and common shell 92
1-pounder top guns, common shell 37

Total number of shots fired 187

There were a number of annoying accidents to parts of the guns of the batteries, but as soon as these were ascertained by actual service (this being the first battle action the ship had had) they were overhauled and practically remedied.

Engagement with batteries at entrance to harbor of Santiago de Cuba, June 22, 1898. Range, 4,000 to 1,500 yards.

Action lasted about an hour. Passed slowly across range from east to west, firing at eastern battery, the Morro, and west battery in succession. The practice was fair. There was a small explosion in the western battery, caused by one of our shells. No great harm was done to the enemy's earthworks, though after the first few minutes his fire perceptibly slackened and later ceased altogether. He returned to his guns, however, as we were drawing off and gave us a few parting shots.

THE GUN-FIRE

Number of shots fired from each gun or turret and kind of ammunition used:—

13-inch turrets: forward, common shell, full charges 1
"   "   after,   "   "   2

    Total 13-inch 3

8-inch turrets: forward, starboard, common shell, full charges 6
8-inch turrets: after, starboard, common shell, full charges 4

    Total 8-inch 10

6-inch guns: starboard, common shell, full charges 11
6-pounder guns: starboard battery, A. P. and common shell 27

    Total number of shots fired 51

The ship's battery worked perfectly, with the exception of two minor troubles with the 13-inch guns.

Engagements with batteries at entrance to harbor of Santiago de Cuba, July 2, 1898. Range, 4,000 to 1,400 yards.

Number of shots fired from each gun or turret and kind of ammunition used:—

13-inch turrets: forward, common shell, full charges 6
"   "   after,   "   "   11

    Total 13-inch 17

8-inch turrets: forward, starboard, common shell, full charges 9
8-inch turrets: forward, port, common shell, full charges 23
8-inch turrets: after, starboard, common shell, full charges 17
8-inch turrets: after, port, common shell, full charges 10

    Total 8-inch 59

6-inch guns, starboard battery 21
"   "   port   "   33

    Total 6-inch 54

6-pounders, both batteries, A. P. and common shell. 443

    Total number of shots fired 573

Engaged about one hour and fifty minutes, stopping occasionally to allow smoke to clear away. Firing at eastern battery and Punta Gorda batteries. The practice was excellent, one gun at eastern battery being dismounted by a 13-inch shell, and the men driven from the others by the fire of the 6-pounders. . . .

Engagement with Admiral Cervera's squadron, July 3, 1898. Range from 4,300 to 2,800 yards.

Number of shots fired from each gun or turret and kind of ammunition used:—

13-inch turrets: forward, common shell, reduced charges	12
13-inch turrets: after, common shell, reduced charges	1
Total 13-inch	13
8-inch turrets: forward, starboard, common shell, full charges	22
8-inch turrets: after, starboard, common shell, full charges	39
Total 8-inch . . .	61
6-inch guns, starboard battery, common shell, full charges	33
6-pounder guns, starboard battery, A. P. and common shell	1,724
6-pounder guns, port battery, A. P. and common shell	20
Total 6-pounder . .	1,744
1-pounder top guns, common shell . . .	25
Total number of shots fired	1,876

Engaged about one hour and twenty minutes, during the first thirty-five minutes of which, or until the Maria Teresa and Oquendo were beached, the firing was very rapid and continuous. Smoke from the 6-pounders interfered considerably with the sighting of the 8-inch guns. Each of the enemy's ships was engaged as she left the entrance, but as they passed to the westward our fire was concentrated upon the two rear ships, the Teresa and Oquendo, and upon the destroyers Furor and Pluton. A number of our large-calibre shells were seen to take effect, and

THE PORT QUARTER-DECK OF THE INFANTA MARIA TERESA

Past Assistant Engineer C. M. Green on deck and Lieutenant B. C. Decker looking for relics

(From photograph by W. G. Cassard on board the Teresa on July 4th)

they were soon set on fire, blown up, or sunk. The ranges were taken from the military top by stadimeter and sextant, and were quite accurate, as there was very little wild shooting, and shot after shot was seen to take effect on the enemy's ships. The guns, mounts, and fittings worked perfectly. It will be noted that reduced charges only were used in the 13-inch guns, and no trouble was experienced with gas check-pads [which had given trouble before with full charges].

Bombardment of the city of Santiago de Cuba from Aguadores, July 10 and 11, 1898. Distance, 8,000 to 9,000 yards.

July 10th, number of shots fired from each gun or turret and kind of ammunition used:—

8-inch guns, starboard after turret, common shell, full charges 4
8-inch guns, starboard forward turret, common shell, full charges 4

Total number of shots fired on July 10th . . . 8

July 11th, port after turret, same ammunition as July 10th 22
July 11th, port forward turret, same ammunition as July 10th 15

Total number of shots fired on July 11th . 37

Total number of shots fired on both days . 45

The bombardment was deliberate, the idea being to fire one 8-inch shell from the ship every two minutes; the bearing and distance of the city were known, and a range was selected on shore over which our gun-pointers were directed to fire. The 13-inch guns were trained to the side opposite the one engaged, in order to list the ship and lessen the strain on the 8-inch mounts. The fire was very effective, though some of the shells failed to burst, a number of houses being destroyed.

       Respectfully,
         S. P. COMLY,
         Lieut. and Ordnance Officer.

THE COMMANDING OFFICER.

COPY OF INDORSEMENT BY THE COMMANDING OFFICER, AUGUST 20, 1898, TO REPORT OF EXPENDITURE OF AMMUNITION TO BUREAU OF ORDNANCE

From my position on the bridge, assisted by the Signal Officer, Lieutenant Dawson, U.S.M.C., and with the Navigator, Lieutenant Comly, directly under me in the conning tower, and a young officer, Cadet Chase, thoroughly trained in taking ranges in the top, I have been able to form a good estimate of our firing in all the engagements the ship has been in. The result of my observation is satisfactory for all of these fights, but in the affair of July 2d, with the batteries, and the action of July 3d, with Cervera's squadron, I have never known such accuracy and rapidity of fire. It will be noted that the firing, which lasted about one hour and fifty minutes, was principally concentrated in the first forty minutes, and the fire during that period even was much interrupted by smoke. During the times of uninterrupted fire ninety shots per minute were delivered, and the accuracy during these periods was remarkable, although the Oquendo and Teresa received the bulk of our most destructive fire. The Vizcaya in the initial stage of the action received considerable damage from the Indiana.

H. C. TAYLOR,
Captain U. S. Navy, Commanding.

CHAPTER VI

THE MARINE GUARD

The Story of the Indiana's Marines in Battle. Report to the Colonel Commandant, U. S. Marine Corps.

U. S. S. INDIANA, *First Rate*,
OFF TOMPKINSVILLE, *September* 1, 1898.

Sir: In accordance with the request contained in the letter of the Colonel Commandant, U. S. Marine Corps, under date of August 9th, I have the honor to submit the following report:

The marines of this ship are stationed for battle as follows: 24 manning port 6-pounder rapid-fire guns on superstructure deck; 20 in powder division passing rapid-fire ammunition; 2 orderlies to commanding officer; 1 signal man; 2 orderlies passing ranges on orlop deck; 1 in central telephone station; 2 in top, assisting in range finding and indicating; 8 on searchlights (at night); 15 in reserve as riflemen, and as supports and reserves for rapid-fire guns.

First Lieutenant W. C. Dawson is stationed on the bridge with the Commanding Officer, acting as Signal Officer.

By direction of the Commanding Officer, I have charge of all the rapid-fire guns on the superstructure and bridge-decks with the exception of two, making in all sixteen guns.

The marines took part in all the engagements in which the ship participated. . . . The bombardments of the city of Santiago de Cuba were carried on by the great guns, and the marines took no part in the firing. In all the picket boats on duty at the mouth of Santiago Harbor there were detachments of marines.

Practically, since a day or two after the destruction of the Maine, this ship has been on a war basis, and all precautions observed in time of war have been carried out. In all of the wearing and wearying watch duty, all war work both in preparation for and during actual warfare, the marines willingly and cheerfully took part, performing the many duties required of them so well that, during the time of preparation and war, there were only two cases of dereliction of duty; and at all times meeting with the approval and gratification of the Commanding Officer, who has stated to me that he regarded our men as the best in the squadron.

I cannot mention specific cases of duty performed in a markedly superior manner when all did so well.

On July 2d, during the attack on the forts at Santiago, the marines did all the firing at the eastern battery and the Morro. This firing was so accurate and controlled as to draw from the Commanding Officer and the officers of other ships strong expressions of admiration and approval. For three days previous to this fight all of the marines, except the orderlies and non-commissioned officers, were with the crew coaling ship, only completing the work at midnight on the 1st of July in time to get under way, leave Guantanamo Bay, and reach Santiago in the early morning, to go into action without time to wash the coal dust off their persons. They went into the fight with such spirit and showed such qualities of discipline and precision as to draw forth a special order from the Commanding Officer commending the seamen and marines for their fine work.

On this occasion the marines fired 570 shots with splendid accuracy.

On the occasion of the destruction of Cervera's fleet the rapid-fire battery of this ship fired 1,744 shots in about 65 minutes. Of this number 1,534 were fired by the guns under my charge, a little more than a third of this number being fired by the marines.

While the marines are stationed at the port battery, and the starboard battery was engaged on that occasion, the fire was so rapid and sustained, the shock of explosion and the blinding smoke from the 8-inch and 6-inch guns were so great, that it was necessary frequently to relieve the crews of the starboard battery with the marines from the port. The only trouble experienced at that time was the difficulty of keeping the men not actually

CAPTAIN LITTLETON W. T. WALLER, COMMANDING MARINE GUARD OF THE INDIANA, CAPTURES TWO PRIZES.

engaged under cover; they were constantly crowding to the guns, waiting for a chance to take part in the action.

The condition of the Oquendo and the Teresa after the action, together with the rapid destruction of the torpedo-boat destroyers, attests to the accuracy of the fire of the rapid-fire batteries. The statement made in Norfolk, by Captain Conchas of the Teresa, to the effect that he could not keep his men at the guns or send messages and orders on account of the terrible fire from the rapid-fire guns of the three eastern ships of the squadron is a further proof of the accuracy and rapidity of the fire of these guns.

Captain Conchas stated, in conversation with civilians, that his ship was destroyed by the fire from the three first ships a few minutes after leaving the channel and turning to the westward.

As I have previously stated, I cannot mention any special instances of extraordinary conduct on the part of the men during the several engagements in which they participated; they have at all times and under all circumstances performed their duties well and faithfully, meeting with the approval of all.

In the case of Lieutenant Dawson I cannot speak of his conduct during any of the actions from personal observation, as he was on the bridge with the Commanding Officer.

In all the preliminaries and preparations for war, Mr. Dawson has been responsible and indefatigable in the discharge of his duties. I cannot speak with too much praise of his capacity and interest.

I must leave to my seniors to say whether or not I performed my duties satisfactorily and well.

Very respectfully,
L. W. T. WALLER,
Captain U. S. M. C., Commanding Marines.

THE COLONEL COMMANDANT, U. S. MARINE CORPS,
Washington, D. C.

Captain Taylor, commanding the Indiana, in a letter to the Navy Department accompanying his indorsement of the foregoing report, suggested that a similar report be obtained from each division of the ship, each of which did its war duty equally well and creditably. In his indorsement Captain Taylor said:

"The conduct of the marines equalled in excellence that of the other divisions of the ship. All divisions of the ship, including marines, behaved admirably in all the various engagements of the war.

"In the destruction of Cervera's fleet the marines fired about five hundred shots from the secondary battery of the ship, about twelve hundred being fired by the seamen division. The smaller number fired by the marines was caused by their having the port battery, while the starboard was engaged. The accuracy of the 6-pounders' fire both from the seamen and the marines was exceptionally good.

"With reference to the marine officers of the Indiana, their conduct was equally deserving high praise and commendation with the other officers of the ship."

CHAPTER VII

STORY OF THE PUNCH BOWL

How it Obtained its Battle Scar. Also, Details of the Havoc caused by the Explosion of One 8-inch Shell from a Spanish Mortar Battery.

ANY event transpiring before Santiago on July 2d or 4th was practically overshadowed by the great battle of July 3d, and in this way some interesting events taking place on those days have been almost unknown to the public. One of the most interesting and exciting things which took place in the war history of the battleship Indiana occurred on the 4th of July, five minutes before midnight. The ship's company had settled down into normal routine of action and feeling after the stirring events of the preceding day, and the thought prevailed that, for us at least, the war was over. But it proved otherwise, and we were yet to receive our greatest damage at the hands of the enemy.

When Admiral Cervera's fleet came out, the Reina Mercedes, a second-class cruiser, had remained behind. This, however, did not cause surprise or anxiety to the American officers, as she was known to be in poor condition, and it was supposed she had remained in the harbor for this reason. But on the night of July 4th at midnight this ship undertook to come out. Opinion seems to be divided as to whether her officers intended sinking her in the channel in imitation of Hobson's feat, or making an effort to reach the open sea and escape and thus surpass Admiral Cervera. Whichever plan was contemplated, the undertaking was most hazardous. There had been no relaxation of vigilance upon the part of the American ships, and at this particular hour the battleship Massachusetts was lying close in to the entrance to the harbor with her searchlights playing up the channel.

The glare of the searchlight of a modern man-of-war is of wonderful penetrating power, and shines like a glowing bar of sunlight reaching out through the darkness and making an avenue of light miles in length.

Suddenly into this beam of light came the black, sinister form of a warship. Just a moment to focus strained vision and make sure and the alarm is given, and the men of the Massachusetts tumble out of their bunks and hammocks and run to their guns, rubbing sleep from their eyes as they go. Now be it remembered that the Massachusetts had not been present at the destruction of the fleet on the day previous, through no fault but the fortunes of war which had put her at Guantanamo coaling ship at the critical hour; therefore when an opportunity did come to engage the enemy she went at the work with a double measure of earnestness as if to get the satisfaction denied her on the day before. Small guns flashed spitefully, and great guns roared and sent volumes of dull red flames, wreathed in a drapery of smoke, leaping from their muzzles.

The hills sent back the crack and roar of the guns, until it seemed that the very elements were warring along the mountain tops and through the valleys below. The pitiless and unsleeping searchlight held the doomed Mercedes within a shining circle alive with flying projectiles, many of which were tearing and penetrating her sides.

All that I have described took place within a very short space of time. As soon as the firing began, Captain Taylor decided that the Indiana, which was lying about two miles southeast of the Morro, should go in and take such part in the action as might be necessary or possible. It was not a question of being willing to engage in a sea-fight at night, but altogether whether the Massachusetts would have completed the job in even the few minutes which must intervene before we could get in position where our guns would bear in the channel. And this is really what happened. When we got near the Massachusetts we found that she had sunk the Reina Mercedes, only the spars and smoke-pipe of that vessel being above the waters of the channel.

And now for the kernel of my story. While the Massachusetts had been firing on the Mercedes, that ship had made but feeble effort to reply, but the guns of the Socapa Battery, on the west

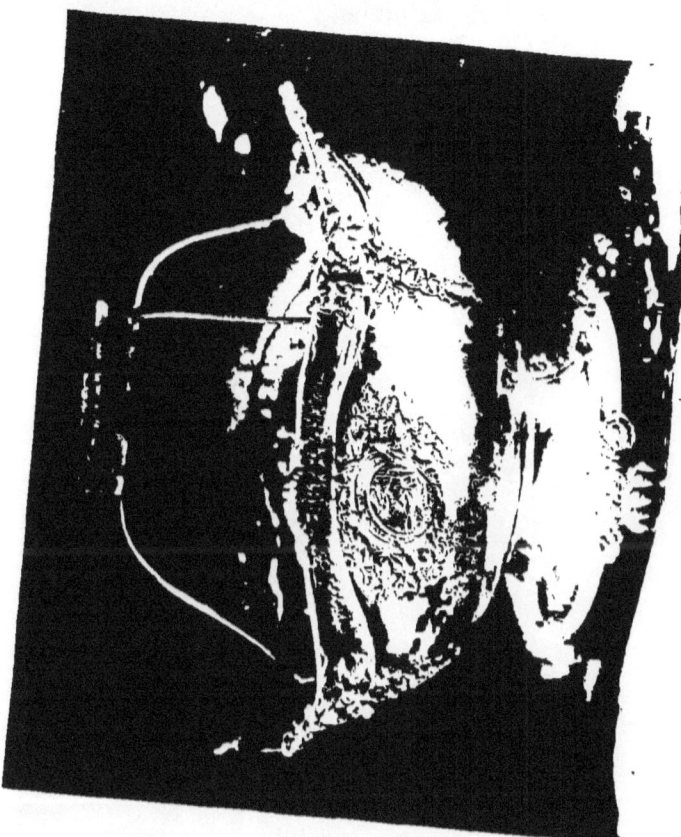

THE BUSH BOMB

[Showing dent made by fragment of shell and the distance on the top and near the seat]

bank of the harbor entrance, had been firing with a briskness unusual for them. Their gunners were aiming at the Massachusetts, and of course they did not strike her; but to our great surprise, and no doubt to their own, one of their 8-inch mortar shells fell plump upon our quarter-deck. It passed through the heavy oaken deck, covered as it was with an iron flash plate, and reaching the berth-deck exploded, flying into a thousand fragments. The noise of the explosion was deafening and the force incredible. The exact point where the explosion took place was just outside the cabin pantry-door, and the destructive force of the explosion extended to the entire cabin and ward-room quarters. Hatch covers were riddled by flying fragments, ladders were converted into kindling wood, bulkheads for a distance of fifty feet were torn and bent, furniture was broken, bookcases overturned, china and glassware smashed and lights extinguished. As the ship's company was at general quarters, none of the officers were in their rooms at the time, which was a most fortunate circumstance, as otherwise some of them would inevitably have been killed or seriously injured. The only person near the shell when it exploded was an apprentice boy—Schoepke—who had gone into that compartment on an errand for one of the officers just before the water-tight doors were closed, and had found his way barred as he sought to return. He was about fifty feet distant from the shell when it exploded, and was thrown down and stunned, but not seriously injured. The compartment in which the explosion occurred was immediately filled with a dense and suffocating smoke, and small fires were started in several rooms. It was but the work of a minute to flood the rooms with water and put out every spark of fire. This was all done quietly and without the least suggestion of excitement or demoralization, although the forts were still firing.

After finding that the Massachusetts had done her work so effectively, the Indiana drew off to her original position without having fired a single gun. When retreat from quarters was sounded we (the officers) went to our rooms, where a sorry spectacle met our gaze. Broken glass, picture frames, ornaments, books, clothing, caps, shoes, etc., were heaped indiscriminately on the floor in about four inches of water. Much of the remainder of the night was spent in trying to bring some degree of order out of this terrible chaos. When day dawned and a closer inspection of the damage done was possible, it was found that a fragment of the shell weighing about two pounds had penetrated the side of one of the oaken chests containing the silverware given the ship by the State of Indiana and dented the punch bowl.

The dented punch bowl is destined to occupy a place of honor in the renovated cabin of the Commanding Officer of the ship, fully marked that future beholders may readily see its significance as a relic of war.

Weeks and months have passed since our experience with this Spanish shell, during most of which time the work of repairing damage done has been going forward, and there now remains only inconspicuous traces of the unwelcome visitor. After witnessing the havoc wrought by this one shell, weighing about two hundred and fifty pounds, we could realize more forcibly the awful experiences of the Spanish ships, overwhelmed as they were by hundreds of exploding shells of all sizes.

SKETCH OF INDIANA'S QUARTER-DECK WHEN SHELL FROM SPANISH BATTERY PENETRATED IT AT MIDNIGHT OF JULY 4th

(Drawn from memory for this book by Carl O. Seivers, Private in Marine Guard, U. S. S. Indiana)

CHAPTER VIII

THE SHIP'S COMPANY AND PRIZES OF WAR

List of the Officers, Crew, and Marines on Board the United States Battleship Indiana at the Time of the Action of July 3, 1898, off Santiago de Cuba, resulting in the Destruction of the Spanish Squadron, composed of the Infanta Maria Teresa (flagship), Almirante Oquendo, Vizcaya, Cristobal Colon, Pluton, and Furor. Also, the Prize Vessels in whose Capture the Indiana was Specially Concerned. The War Volunteers.

OFFICERS

Captain.—Henry Clay Taylor.
Lieutenant-Commander.—John Augustus Rodgers.
Lieutenants.—Samuel Pancoast Comly, Richard Henderson, Roy Campbell Smith, Frederick Lincoln Chapin.
Lieutenants, Junior Grade.—Benton Clark Decker, Thomas Washington.
Ensigns.—Percy Napier Olmsted, William Reynolds Cushman.
Naval Cadets.—Gilbert Chase, Arthur St. Clair Smith, Walter Maxwell Falconer, Willis McDowell, Charles Truesdale Owens, Ernest Clinton Keenan, Cyrus Willard Cole, Herbert Heard Evans, Frank Pinckney Helm, Edgar Brown Larimer, Charles Edwin Morgan, Samuel Brown Thomas, Daniel Pratt Mannix.
Surgeon.—Nelson MacPherson Ferebee.
Assistant Surgeon.—George Dayton Costigan.
Paymaster.—Reah Frazer.
Chief Engineer.—George Cowie.
Passed Assistant Engineers.—Harry Hall, Robert Salmond Talbot, Carl Melville Green.

Assistant Engineers.—Roscoe Charles Moody, Daniel Mershon Garrison.
Chaplain.—William Gilbert Cassard.
Captain, United States Marine Corps.—Littleton Waller Tazewell Waller.
First Lieutenant, United States Marine Corps.—William Charles Dawson.
Pay Clerk.—John Wright Caum.
Boatswain.—James Dowling.
Gunner.—George Lincoln Mallery.
Acting Carpenter.—George William Alexander Bailey.

ENLISTED MEN

Chief Master-at-Arms.—Richard Joseph Keating.
Chief Boatswain's Mate.—Michael Corlos.
Chief Gunner's Mate.—Thomas Stockdale Aveson.
Chief Quartermaster.—Charles Eble.
Chief Machinists.—William King McCall, Emmanuel Salvator, James Kavanagh, Robert Hilldof Lawson, James White.
Chief Carpenter's Mate.—Henry James Wirtz.
Chief Yeomen.—Francis Hamilton, Edward Roche Manley, Charles Elmer Murray, William Martin Gorham.
Apothecary.—Charles Ellis Alexander.
Master-at-Arms, First Class.—Frank John Allen.
Boatswain's Mates, First Class.—Anton Tiedemann, John Costin, Frank Norris, Samuel Canavan.
Gunner's Mates, First Class.—Ernest Schuldt, Harry Dahis, Frank Daily, George Alexander Stevens, Charles Alfred Goodwin, Ulysses Grant Chipman, Edward Murphy, Joseph Koch.
Gunner's Captain, First Class.—Albert Julius Svensson.
Machinists, First Class.—Bernard Christiansen, Philip Rack, William James Lee, James Phillip Winkle, Charles William Henry Ehler.
Boilermakers.—William Francis Creswell, Michael Joseph Miller, John Wesley Glover, Peter Anderson.
Blacksmiths.—Stephen Raybold, Carl Frederick Richardson, Lawrence Mansen.

Plumber and Fitter.—Timothy Francis Mitchell.
Sailmaker's Mate.—James Johnson.
Water Tenders.—Carl Dahl, Michael Horgan, Thomas Holt, John Geary, Thomas Clancy, James Toole.
Yeoman, First Class.—Henry Hayman.
Master-at-Arms, Second Class.—Charles Henry Pratt.
Boatswain's Mates, Second Class.—Charles Forster, Charles Bauer, George Winfield Demarest.
Gunner's Mates, Second Class.—Robert Patterson, Robert Beatty, Sydney William Garrett, Charles August Holmberg, Henry Downey, John Laurell, William Detmers, William Lindley Fieldhouse.
Quartermasters, Second Class.—Charles Lund, James Golden.
Machinists, Second Class.—DeWitt Clinton Dixson, Luke Francis Brennan, William Herzberg, William Christie Leonard, Clifford Cabell Johnston, Joseph Augustus Nangler, Felix John O'Malley, Julius Poulson, Matthias August Thormahlen, Benjamin Franklin Wallace, Frank Henry Zinke.
Oilers.—Michael Haley, John Lyons, Robert Quinn, Alfred Pfeiffer, John Sullivan, William McLean, Ludwig Wilhelm Dahl, Ellwood Mason Rowland.
Yeoman, Second Class.—Howard Asa Kimball.
Master-at-Arms, Third Class.—James Joseph Generson.
Coxswains (Steam Launch).—Adolf Holm, Magnus Carlsson.
Coxswains.—John Conrad Lindberg, James Parks, Philip Sheridan, Karl Forsborn, Bernt Wallentin Lind, Gustav Sauf, William Burke, Carl Oskar Magnussen, John Stephen Daley, Arnold Sauer.
Gunner's Mates, Third Class.—Alexander Coffey, Pitter Sjorgren, Michael Joseph Roskey, Henry Tobina, Frank Danks, Andrew Ludwigson, John Alvin Dry, John Nordstrom.
Quartermasters, Third Class.—William Dobito Gunn, Arthur Louis Stehle.
Carpenter's Mate, Third Class.—Arthur Frank Gentsch.
Painters.—William Joseph Prettyman, Joseph Kearney, Hans Schroeder, Samuel Joseph Francis Bradley.
Seamen.—Thomas McMahon, Louis Hansen, John Dunn, William Knut Armstrong, Charles Edward Thomas, James Andrew Coffin, William Walker, John Quevedo, Frank Plotos, Jens Ludal

Walle, Edward Frank Jackson, Frodig Forsborn, Hjalmar Nordstrom, Anders Henry Jonsson, George Monroe Wells, John Alex Haapanen, Ernest Wallace Larkin, Lewis Sequeland, James Joseph Aylward, Edward Albert Evers, James Richard Mendelssohn, Earle Wayne Redman, Conrad Johnson, Vincent Tobin, Joseph Baker Hedenger, Gustav Svendson, Edward Brodd, Abraham Tabler Angell, Nikla Bendixsen, Frank Johnsen, Frank Keeler, Alfin Albert Green, Lars Mandipis Torkelson, Halfden Bernard Hansen, Michael Farrell, John Bently, Otto Andresen, Ole Olsen, John Michel Niles, Antoni Michell, Otto Lehman, Bert Vernon, Jakob Oorburg, William Henry Humphrey, John Evans, Jakob Halvorsen, Erick Lindstrom, John Alexsanter Lehtonen, Frank Dressler, George Washington Myers, John Warden Taylor, Charles Von Warren, Elmer Edward Groff, Jesse Alexander Parenteau, Edgar Weems Smith, Henry Jones, Harry Erben Campbell, Peter John Boyesen, Carl Fogelberg, Charles Thomas Brookman, James Kelly, Harry Augustus Williams, Carl Halvorsen, Jens Berggreen, Edward Livingston Gill, William Herlitz, Charles Fred Hubert, Jason Wright Jones, Charles Johnsen, Olaf Lindseth.

Seaman, Captain of Hold.—Charles Perkins.

Apprentices, First Class.—John Sperle, Jr., Christopher Emold, Joseph Arthur Michael Pippin, Duke B. Starr, Charles Frank Weber, Alfred Franklin Kelly, William Clarence Vail, William Kramer, John Lewis Fitch, Roy Stewart Ranier, William Howard Leitch, Edward Kendrick Dean, Martin Aloysius Owens, Joseph Dana Lindsay, Clifford Hunter Robb, Leroy Rodd, Catesby Jones, Michael John Braughel, Elmer Alexander Dey, George Joseph Hartman, Calvin Mengle, James Robert Crawford, Jesse Franke Spink, Vincent De Paul Garrigan, Charles Stephen Schopke, Dennis Curtin, Albert Rudolph Ribas, Harry Buckley Boies, Thomas Francis Burns, George Stanley Bergantz, David St. John Greer, Thomas Richard Sandidge, Duncan Herbert Sell.

Firemen, First Class.—James Monahan, James Reed, William Knice, Ole Bergstrom Mortensen, Gust Green, Robert John Alford, Frank Rench, James Michael McCann, William Garrett Moore, Richard Finn, Carl Christian Jensen, Henry Hubert

ASSISTANT ENGINEER GARRISON INTERESTS TWO OF THE SHIP'S MASCOTS WHILE THE CHAPLAIN TAKES A "SNAP"

"Blanco," the kitten, was gathered up by the Chaplain at Key West, early in the campaign. He purchased this then most forlorn bit of cathood of a small boy for twenty-five cents. During the progress of the war, Blanco thrived and grew fat and happy. During the battle at Santiago she secreted herself in the brig.

"Nan," the goat, was captured at Hampton Roads before the war, and waxed fat and inquisitive in the atmosphere of powder smoke. She likewise developed a liking for tobacco ashes even more pronounced than her taste for newspapers. On coming north after the war she allowed her tastes to be elevated and would eat only pages of magazines—and tobacco ashes. During the action of July 3d, she had a place of refuge in the sick-bay, under the surgeon's operating table.

Fehrenschield, Edward Baertschigar, Daniel Phelan, Jeremiah Mourley, Archibald McCoy, Edward Mason, Owen Kirwan.

Ordinary Seamen.—William Henry Bayle, Charles Lawrence, Joseph Miller, Charles Bernard, George Farrell, Arthur Edward Arnold, Charles Samm, Marshall Bertin Atwell, Carl Erick Anderson, Junius Johnson, Joseph Mulhall, Francis Joseph Hammell, David Bain, Peter Downey, William Buchanan May, John Harvey Stocks, James Wallace MacLean, Thomas Henry Murray, Ralph Tilghman Fisher, John Thomas Powers, Julius Grant Craw, Joseph Foy Chapman, James Willard Ford, Joseph Constant Gagnon, Otto Helmerichs, James Robert Hanham, Joseph Keating, Edward Wilhelm Levan, Peter Le Engle, John Meyers, Calvin Seymour Miller, John Manley, Lydick Johannes Johansson, William John Smith, George Bostwick, Joseph Stephen Rose, Edward Winther, Charles Martin Henry Olsen, Marius Rasmussen, Earle Stuart Dean, David Jamieson, Joseph Chesborough Pretti, William Adam Schwabe, Robert Adams, Konrad Haake, William Britton, Wilbert Hayes Elliott, James Sliney, Robert Trinlett, William Peter Williams, Patrick Kirwin, George Fox, Luther Slate, Walter Leonard Graves, Edward Watson Hall, Androas Edward Hernansen, Otto Rudolf, Robert Edward Weber, Arthur Boos, James Farrell, John Grant Rotherham, Daniel Elighter Stapleton, Edward Francis Maybaum, Charles Henry Colburn, August Anderson, Jacob Adolph Loeb, Lindsay MacLeish.

Apprentices, Second Class.—Francis Joseph Kane, Charles Frederick Henderson, Eugene Fatton, John Francis Dolan, James Edward Powers, Edward Aloysius Fee, Theodore Louis Pieper, John Harrison, Richard Carter, Michael Joseph Wilkinson, Charles Augustus Lyman, George Henry O'Donoghue, Frederick Hoenstel Field, David Frederick Mead, Frank Richard Stone, Henry Taylor, Frank Leslie Gransbury, Ernest Eldridge Comstock, John Joseph Howe, Henry Llewellyn Bixbee, John Dick Rockefeller, Hudson Arthur Steele, Maurice Doherty, John Koehler, Austin Wilden Lee, John Capell, Howard Gogus Thomas, Arthur Illston Haines, William Henry Heistand, Clarence Bernard Kyle, John Broadfoot Macfarlane, Edward William McGregor, William Garland Allan, Charles Leonard Seifert.

Firemen, Second Class.—Thomas Dryhurst, William Bowman, John Lynch, John Casey, Frank McNulty, Arthur Percy Green, Jacob Peter Windness, William Ward, James O'Brine, Edward Augustus Donovan, Harry Francis King, John Eberhart, Peter Claborn Rushing, Charles Rife, Gustaf Aroid Person, Michael Cowles, William Delaney, John Edward Moran, John Stafford, John Thompson, Edward Walsh, Charles Herbert Penny, George Albert Hewitt, John Mitchell, Charles Anderson, Patrick Flood, Patrick Gallivan, William Glynn, Anthony Murphy.

Shipwrights.—Emanuel Sarsfield, Charles Leishman.

Bugler.—Wayne Abbott.

Landsmen.—Alfred Sipe, Charles Lee, Martin Van Buren Webber, Joseph Siemele, John Beaghen, Edward Turley, Edward William Ryan, Edward Harvey Hammond, John Hilbert Meehan, Nicholas Keppler, James Joseph Crotty, Victor Johnson, Michael Kennedy, Jeremiah Donovan, Florence Klinck Rauftle, Frank Mogridge.

Landsman (Jack of Dust).—Henry Burkhardt.

Coal Passers.—Harry Johannes, William Martin Haggerty, William Tilly, Isaac Threwitt, Charles Dexter Cole, Frank Wyatt, Charles Smith, John Lynch, Charles Britton, William Curran, William Henry Cooke, Timothy Cahill, John Theodore Sybrandi, John Hazel Call, James Carr, Charles Henry Williams, Louis Patrick Brown, Frank Price, Michael McCann, John David Collins, Anthony Drolett, James Henry Dougherty, William Goldsmith Duff, Robert Jones, Daniel Elliott, Charles William Williams, Fred Langley, Robert McMullen, James Fox, Patrick Sharkey, Adrian Gothus Teel, Mikel Mesment Roach, Henry Lewis, Victor Emanuel Roney, Thomas O'Brien, Peter Hourihan, Edward Kenney, Fred Tate, William Frank Buchanan, Thomas McDonough, Daniel Dempsey, Edward Sheehy, John Springer, August See, James Tucker.

Baymen.—Thomas Joseph Gray, George Kingwell.

Cabin Steward.—John Gibson.

Cabin Cook.—John Andrew Cutrell.

Ward-room Steward.—Charles Edward Wilson.

Ward-room Cook.—Edward Antonio Dos Santos.

Steerage Steward.—Massa Tobe.

Steerage Cook.—Aiychi Shima.
Warrant Officer's Steward.—William Preston Moore.
Warrant Officer's Cook.—James McCullough.
Ship's Cook, First Class.—James Joseph Conners.
Ship's Cooks, Second Class.—Daniel Collins, Herbert William Doggrell, Frank White Clark.
Ship's Cooks, Third Class.—John Thomas Welch, Henry William Meitzler.
Ship's Cooks, Fourth Class.—Maurice O'Connor, Patrick Fogarty, James Joseph Hamilton.
Mess Attendants.—John Richard Elsey, James Spratley, Alexander Albert King, Edward Everitte Seavey, George Theodore Poste, James Alexander Manning, Alfred Cornelius Black, Cornelius Henry Tatem, Jen Komaten, Naka Shima.

MARINES

First Sergeant.—Charles Gamborg Andresen.
Sergeants.—Carl Schneider, Daniel Moriarty Delaney, John Joseph Kelly, Fred Hodson, Leon Wesley Mayshaw, James Duffy, Frank Sweeney.
Fifer.—John Onesine Dusett.
Drummer.—Edwin Milton Thomasson.
Privates.—Patrick Barry, Robert Emil Bensler, William Clayton Blackiston, William Oliver Buyer, Michael Brooks, Thomas Canfield, Richard Clynes, George Colter, Frank Davis, Mike Downey, Michael Downs, Francis Ignatious Duffy, John Edward Ely, Albert Gosling, Ethan Nathan Hescock, August Holmberg, Denis Looney, Adolph Mitscherling, Daniel O'Brien, Timothy O'Brien, George Raby Orr, Edward Frederick Russell, Theodore Valentine Sherman, Alvin Thomas Shepard, Francis Sweeney, John Daniel Showalter, Michael Butler, Michael Kelly, Benard Temple Robinson, Eugene William Marcy, Alfred Lawrence Walsh, Gustav Pingel, James Clancy, Patrick Maher, Patrick Dunne, Edward Mickle Miles, Jason Sanford Verge, Edgar Poe Crouse, Charles Adolph Arians, Charles Rolle, Charles Howard, Andrew Gunter, Thomas Hunter Jernigan, Charles Nolan, Rutherford Hayes Porter, James Julius Ryan, Nelson Jerome Hurd,

Joseph Malachi Kelly, Walter Lawrence O'Neal, Joseph Samuel King, Thomas Francis Farrington, Robert Grant, Thomas Gilligan, Patrick Harkins, William Hecker, Frederick Baker Howes, James Mahoney, Henry Daniel Miller, Theodore McClenon, Frank Martin Pahl, Louis Schmiedt, Carl Ohlson Sievers, John William Tutcher, William John Taylor, Joseph Patrick Williams.

Prizes of War

The Indiana was interested particularly in the capture of six prizes of war:

No. 1. April 22.—The Spanish steamer Buena Ventura, sighted by the Indiana and photographs taken. The Indiana was within easy gun range and within signal distance of the Nashville at the time she made the capture.

No. 2. April 25.—The Spanish steamer Panama, captured off Havana during the blockade of that port, by the U. S. S. Mangrove, assisted by the Indiana. Boatswain Dowling fired a 6-pounder shot across the steamer's bow, which aided materially in inducing her to haul down her colors and surrender. A prize crew was sent aboard from the Indiana in charge of Cadet Falconer.

No. 3. May 5, about 9 A.M.—A Spanish barkentine, the Frasquito, captured by the Montgomery off the north coast of Cuba. The Indiana was within easy gun range and signal distance.

No. 4. May 5, about 1.30 P.M.—A Spanish brigantine, the Lorenzo, captured by the Montgomery off the north coast of Cuba, by order of the flagship. The Indiana was within easy signal distance and within easy gun range.

No. 5. July 3.—The fleet commanded by Admiral Cervera. In the destruction of the Maria Teresa, Oquendo, Vizcaya, and the torpedo-boat destroyer Pluton this ship claims special credit.

No. 6. July 4.—The destruction of the Reina Mercedes. The Indiana was standing by ready to render any assistance that might be needed, and was hit by a Spanish shell from a shore battery while doing so.

The War Volunteers

Several volunteer officers were assigned to the Indiana at various times during the war, most of them being in the engineer department.

During the time of the Santiago campaign, including the days of the bombardment and the battle with Cervera's fleet, some sixty members of the Illinois Naval Militia, who had entered the navy when war began, served on board the Indiana, with credit to themselves and the State organization from which they came. After the fleet returned to New York, the latter part of August, they were transferred to the receiving ship Vermont at the New York Navy Yard, and then sent home with other men of the Illinois Naval Militia, who had done like service on other ships, to be honorably discharged.

There were also on board the Indiana about one hundred one-year men, or volunteers for the war, whose services were retained some time after the Illinois men were sent home, the Navy Department having decided that their services could not be dispensed with before the treaty of peace was officially ratified.

The Relief Boats' Crews

With Lieutenant Decker was Coxswain Carl O. Magnusson and the following boat's crew: L. Hansen, C. Johnson, Bergreen, D. B. Starr, W. H. Bayle, A. Sipe, Hanham, Haake, Lindsey, Wilkinson, Donaghue, D. F. Mead, F. Johnson, C. Bernard.

Ensign Olmsted was in charge of the relief boat, with Coxswain Philip Sheridan and the following crew: Maybaum, Herlitz, Jones, Halvorsen, Burns, J. Farrell, Forsborn, Rodd, G. Farrell.

CHAPTER IX

THE INTERNAL MECHANISM

Miscellaneous Information about the Indiana, showing the Varied Industries carried on on Board a Battleship, the Guns and the Ammunition, and Other Items of Information.

A MODERN battleship of the Indiana type is a town in itself. Almost all branches of industry are represented. The following list of the rates held by the men and the number of each rate on board the Indiana will give to the civilian some idea of the varied knowledge required to operate such a fighting machine.

U. S. S. INDIANA, COMPLEMENT ON WAR FOOTING

Established by Order, April 7, 1898

SEAMAN BRANCH

Chief Master-at-Arms	1
Master-at-Arms, First Class	1
" " " Second "	1
" " " Third "	1
Chief Boatswain's Mate	1
Boatswain's Mates, First Class	4
" " Second "	4
Coxswains	12
Chief Gunner's Mate	1
Gunner's Mates, First Class	8
" " Second "	8
" " Third "	8
Chief Quartermaster	1
Quartermaster, First Class	1

THE INTERNAL MECHANISM 131

Quartermaster, Second Class 1
Quartermasters, Third " 2
Seamen 101
Ordinary Seamen 40
Apprentices 46
Landsmen 34

    Total 276

ARTIFICER BRANCH

Chief Carpenter's Mate 1
Carpenter's Mate, First Class 1
" " Third " 1
Shipwrights 2
Blacksmith 1
Sailmaker's Mate 1
Plumber and Fitter 1
Painters 2

    Total 10

ENGINE-ROOM FORCE

Chief Machinists 5
Machinists, First Class 5
Boilermaker 1
Blacksmith 1
Coppersmith 1
Water Tenders 6
Machinists, Second Class 5
Oilers 8
Firemen, First Class 26
  " Second " 14
Coal Passers 51

    Total 123

SPECIAL BRANCH

Hospital Steward	1
Yeoman, Equipment	1
Commissary	1
Engineers'	1
Commanding Officer	1
Pay	1
First Class	1
Second "	1
Buglers, or Apprentices for	1
Hospital Apprentices	2
Total	11

MESSMAN BRANCH

Cabin Steward	1
" Cook	1
Mess Attendant	1
Ward-room Steward	1
" Cook	1
Mess Attendants	8
Steerage Steward	1
" Cook	1
Mess Attendants	3
Warrant Officers' Steward	1
" " Cook	1
Ship's Cooks, First Class	1
" " Second "	3
" " Third "	2
" " Fourth "	3
Total	29
Total Complement of Crew	449
Marine Guard	75
	524

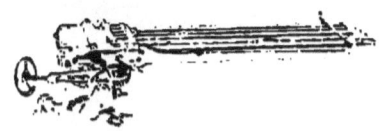

NORDENFELDT MACHINE GUN

Taken from military top of Admiral Cervera's flagship by
Chief Gunner's Mate Aveson

RIFLE BARREL

From wreck of Spanish warship

THE MAIL ORDERLY

BACKBOARD

From small boat belonging to the Pluton

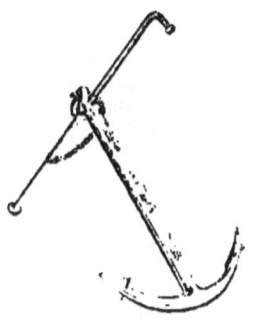

BOAT ANCHOR

From Spanish flagship Maria Teresa

**SPANISH GOLD COINS ON BASE
OF MELTED SILVER**

From the Maria Teresa

On war basis : 524 men, 36 officers. Divided as follows : On deck, seaman's branch, 276 men ; engine-room force, 123 men, 6 officers ; special branch, 11 men ; artificer branch, 10 men ; messman branch, 30 men ; marine guard, 75 men, 2 officers.

BATTERY

Main Battery.—Four 13-inch, Mark I, hydraulic mount B. L. rifles, mounted in pairs, in two turrets, one forward, one aft. Armor-piercing shells weigh 1,100 pounds. Full charges of powder weigh 550 pounds.

Eight 8-inch, Mark IV, spring return mount B. L. rifles, mounted in pairs in turrets, two forward, two aft. Armor-piercing shells weigh 250 pounds. Full powder charges weigh 125 pounds.

Four 6-inch rapid-firing, spring return B. L. rifles, mounted on pedestal mounts, in barbettes, two on starboard side and two on port side, amidships. Shells weigh 100 pounds and powder charges (smokeless powder) 26 to 28 pounds each. (These guns were installed in the Indiana in November, 1898, and were the first guns on board to use smokeless powder exclusively. Smokeless powder was used to a limited extent in the old-style 6-inch guns, of which these take the place, during some actions of the war.)

Secondary Battery.—Twenty 6-pounder Hotchkiss rapid-fire rifles, mounted on cage and rail mounts.

Six 1-pounder Hotchkiss rapid-fire rifles, heavy ; two in fighting top ; four (boat pieces) mounted on top of 8-inch turrets.

One 1-pounder Maxim-Nordenfeldt automatic gun, mounted on after bridge rail.

Four Whitehead torpedo-tubes and six torpedoes.

Total number of guns of all calibres, 43. Total weight of ammunition carried on board, about 425 tons.

WEIGHT OF GUNS

Each 13-inch breech-loading rifle, about 61 tons, exclusive of mount, etc. ; each 8-inch breech-loading rifle, about 13 tons, exclusive of mount, etc. ; each 6-inch rapid-fire breech-loading rifle, about 2½ tons, exclusive of mount, etc.; each 6-pounder rapid-fire breech-loading rifle, about 792 pounds; each 1-pounder rapid-fire breech-loading rifle, about 297 to 497 pounds, including mounts.

Total weight of metal that can be thrown at one discharge, main and secondary batteries, 7,200 pounds.

Armor

(Nickel steel.) Length of special armor belt at water-line, 150 feet; thickness of belt, thickest part, 18 inches; depth of belt, 7 feet 6 inches; armor of 13-inch turrets, 15 inches; armor of 8-inch turrets, 6 inches; armor around barbettes and 6-inch battery, 5 inches. Other armor of ship, varying from 5 to 14 inches.

Engines

Horse-power, two engines, 10,000; main boilers, 4; auxiliary boilers, 2; electric dynamos, 3. Total number of engines of all sorts on board the Indiana, 86. As follows: 2 main propelling engines; 2 main air pumps; 2 main circulating pumps; 2 auxiliary air and circulating pumps; 2 main reversing engines; 2 main turning engines; 1 workshop engine; 6 evaporator and distilling pumps; 1 oil pump; 2 feed, fire, and bilge pumps; 2 fire and bilge pumps; 2 water-service pumps; 4 main feed pumps for main boilers; 4 auxiliary feed pumps for main boilers; 2 main feed pumps for auxiliary boilers; 2 auxiliary feed pumps for auxiliary boilers; 10 forced-draft blowers; 2 ventilating blowers for engine-room; 4 ventilating blowers for ship; 4 ash-hoisting engines; 3 dynamo engines; 1 steering engine; 2 13-inch turret engines; 4 8-inch turret engines; 1 ice machine; 1 windlass and capstan engine; 6 winches (2 electric); 2 hydraulic pumps; 2 accumulators; 2 air compressors; 1 pump for waste-water tank; 2 steam cutter propelling engines; 2 steam cutter feed pumps.

Ship's bunkers will take about 1,600 tons of coal. The crew can coal ship at the rate of 700 tons a day under favorable conditions.

Bower anchors weigh 14,120 and 15,000 pounds each. Bower chains are 120 fathoms long.

Length of ship on water-line, 248 feet; extreme breadth, 69 feet 3 inches; normal displacement, 10,200 tons; normal draught, 24 feet; draught with full stores and coal supply, 26 feet 4 inches; total displacement, all stores, etc., aboard, 11,403 tons.

CHAPTER X

NEWSPAPER NOTICES

Press Mention of the Indiana and Matters concerning the Ship. Some Words in Appreciation of Attention Received.

From the time the battleship Indiana received its name the people of the State of Indiana have taken a lively and continual interest in the ship and her doings. This has been shown in the presentation of the elegant and valuable silver service and library by the citizens of the State, and by the attention given the ship by the newspapers of the State. The Indianapolis *News* has been conspicuous in this respect, but by no means the only one to devote liberal space from time to time to the ship's affairs. Lieutenant W. H. Elliott, manager of the New Castle *Courier*, served during the war as a volunteer naval officer, and he saw to it that his paper always kept its readers informed as to the doings of the State's namesake in the Navy. The officers and men of the United States ship Indiana appreciate the attention given them in this way, and anything concerning the State of Indiana interests them.

As a sample of the newspaper notices referred to, the following from the Indianapolis *News* of October 4, 1898, are reproduced into this book. The first is an editorial notice, the second is a portion of an article written by an Indiana man who visited the ship after she came to New York at the close of the war.

INDIANA TO THE FRONT

"Yesterday we presented the official report of the commander of the Resolute, which shows that the Indiana was the first to receive the fire of the Spanish fleet as each of the boats came out of the harbor, and that it was her own effective fire that first reached the Maria Teresa and the Vizcaya, while it was one of her shells that 'did' for the torpedo-boat Furor; and all the while her secondary battery was playing havoc. . . .

"In short, the vastly important part that our namesake bore in this great battle was something to cause additional pride. A supplemental report of this kind from a correspondent of the *News* is given elsewhere in to-day's issue—in a story of a vjsit to the Indiana as she lies in the Brooklyn Navy Yard. Her captain is a fighter, not a talker, and a modest man withal. So the glory which has come to the Oregon and the Brooklyn, while it may not be diminished, can have for companionship the glory which the Indiana won in the same battle. Thus the goodly State seems to be forging ahead.

"The noted sculptor, George Grey Barnard, whose great work is so known and recognized on both sides of the sea that he has been called the greatest of living sculptors, is identified with Indiana in a way, as is told in the very interesting account of the home of his parents at Madison. When it comes to good things, from authors and artists to battleships, Indiana seems to be at the front and up and doing."

Another Distinction

"New York, October 1.—From the first it has been apparent that the battleship Indiana is a credit and an honor to the State whose name she bears. In structure, mechanical, and technical points she is not surpassed by any vessel in the service. The naval engagements of the recent war have been limited in number, but the Indiana has been conspicuous in the only important actions in this hemisphere—the bombardment of San Juan and the destruction of Cervera's fleet. Captain Taylor has proved himself a commander of distinction and bravery, and the men behind the Indiana's guns have demonstrated their daring and efficiency.

"The Indiana is now in the famous dry dock No. 3 in the Brooklyn Navy Yard, the only dry dock in this country large enough to hold securely this giant battleship. Here thousands visit the marine fighter every day. It is down in the records at Washington that the Indiana did work unexcelled by any other ship in action.

"Gradually there is being established the magnificent record of one of the finest battleships and the bravest and most proficient set of officers and seamen in the world. Indiana has reason to be proud of them. This record, for instance, shows officially that the Indiana fired 1,876 shots during the hour and a half of general action at Santiago, from the time Cervera's fleet came out of the harbor till our shells had sunk or beached the Maria Teresa, Oquendo, Vizcaya, Pluton, and Furor.

"For his bravery and ability in this action Captain Taylor has been advanced five numbers in rank, and his executive officer for the same conduct has received the same reward. Admiral Sampson, after Cervera's destruction, placed the Indiana to guard the entrance to the Santiago Harbor, and meet and destroy any other Spanish warships attempting to escape. It was a triumphant moment.

"Another distinction which belongs to our ship was that of being one of the first to send a chaplain and a surgeon ashore with a detail to look after the prisoners. They landed near the burning hulk of the Maria Teresa, not two hundred feet away, which, under the towering proportions of a great warship, is practically beneath it. Here the brave Indiana officers and sailors ministered to the dying and wounded under more trying and dangerous circumstances than at any moment of the preceding hour and a half of battle. The Spanish had deserted the Maria Teresa with her guns loaded but undischarged. The heat of the burning hulk exploded these charges, and exploded the fixed ammunition on deck as well as the stores in the magazines. It rained a constant fusillade about the Indiana's relief party, but they never wavered.

. . . . .

"The character of the men manning the Indiana is evidenced in the fact that when Captain Taylor ordered the men to the guns they went with a cheer, not with smiling satisfaction and muttered eagerness, but with a hearty, rousing cheer. Grimy and sooty with the dirt of battle, half naked, perspiring, exhausted after the action, they hailed joyfully the Captain's word that another warship was on the horizon, perhaps the Pelayo. ' When that ship showed the Austrian flag,' said a Jackie on the Indiana, ' we were the sorest lot of tars in water; no, not even excepting the beaten blokies in the Spanish wrecks.'

. . . . .

"The men on the Indiana are proud of the ship's name, and feel an affectionate kinship for the citizens of the State. The men and their gallant Captain deserve well of the State and the citizens.

"No State in the Union is better represented in the Navy by a ship of better type or efficiency or officers and crew of greater gallantry and bravery than Captain Taylor, his men, and the battleship Indiana."

From Photograph by Harry K. Corbett.

AN ENTHUSIASTIC WELCOME.

A view of the decks of the Massachusetts, a sister ship of the Indiana, after the fleet came north, showing the manner in which the civilian visitors crowded on board. This was chiefly women on the Indiana and the other ships of Admiral Sampson's fleet for a week, after they reached New York, the 1st of August.

As a Spanish Officer Saw It

As shedding a little light on the events of July 3d, the following extract from one of the publications of the Naval Intelligence Office, recently issued, is reprinted here. The document tells the story of the battles and capitulation of Santiago, ending with a diary of a Spanish naval officer (Lieutenant Muller), which tells the story vividly from his standpoint.

" At six o'clock in the evening of [July 3d] Miguel Lopez, the pilot of the Maria Teresa, Cervera's flagship, arrived and told of the catastrophe. Then Lieutenant Muller, being bent on getting all the news for his diary, sought out Lopez and got him to tell his story. This is the way Lieutenant Muller tells it :
"' Miguel Lopez, who is cool-headed and daring on land as well as on sea, said to me about as follows : " I was in the forward tower by the side of Admiral Cervera, who was as calm as though he had been at anchor, in his own cabin, and was observing the channel and the hostile ships and only said these words : 'Pilot, when can we shift the helm ?' He had reference to turning to starboard, which could only be done after we had passed Diamante Bank. After a few seconds he said : 'Pilot, advise me when we can shift the helm.' ' I will advise you, Admiral,' I answered.
"'" A few moments later I said : ' Admiral, the helm may be shifted now.'
"'" In a moment the Admiral, without shouting, without becoming excited, as calm as usual, said, 'To starboard !' and the next minute, ' Fire !'
"'"At the same moment simultaneously the two guns of the turret and those of the port battery fired on a ship which seemed to me to be the Indiana.
"'" I thought the ship was sinking. I cannot tell you, Don José, all that passed. By this time there were already many dead and wounded in the battery, because they had been firing on us for some time, and I believe that in spite of the water that was in the ship she was already on fire then. The Admiral said to me, ' Good-by, pilot ; go now, and be sure to let them pay you, because you have earned it well,' and he continued to give orders." ' "

FROM "THE ILLUSTRATED LONDON NEWS"
(*October* 15, 1898)

"While there was but one life lost on the side of the United States in the naval battle with Cervera's fleet off Santiago de Cuba, the battleships have many scars to indicate how hot must have been the cannonading by the Spaniards. One of the most singular freaks of a mortar-shell was that which burst in the ward-room passage of the battleship Indiana. A fragment from this shell, five and one-half inches long, weighing about five pounds, struck the massive punch bowl belonging to the solid silver service which Messrs. Tiffany & Company of New York made for the vessel, and which was presented to it by the people of the State of Indiana in whose honor it was named. The bowl received the blow on the body, where the seal of the State forms the central portion of a rich decoration. The seal is still there, but not as the artist designed it; for it now forms a part of a large, irregular indentation, which, though destroying the symmetry of the beautiful bowl, does not impair its usefulness. As a memento of the Indiana's participation in the battle, the injury to the bowl has a thousand times enhanced its value, and that the honorable distinction it gives to it may be perpetuated, the Messrs. Tiffany are having the scar properly inscribed, and the piece of shell mounted upon the bowl in such a way that it may be lifted off like a cover, and the bowl used when desired. Upon the inside of the bowl, over the bulged-in part, will be engraved or etched the following inscription: 'Made by a fragment of a mortar-shell fired from the Socapa Battery, Santiago de Cuba, which burst in the ward-room passage of the U. S. Battleship Indiana, midnight, July 4, 1898.'

"This punch bowl is one of the largest and richest pieces of the Indiana's silver service. It stands eleven inches high, measures nineteen and one-half inches across the top, and has a capacity of four gallons. It is lined with gold, and the decorations, which are all in repoussé work, include the State seal of Indiana, the famous soldiers' and sailors' monument in the city of Indianapolis, and the principal flora and trees of the State, all interwoven into a highly artistic and symbolic design. The entire silver service of the battleship Indiana consists of about forty pieces, including candelabra, tea set, waiter, etc., all of sterling silver. It weighs about two hundred pounds, and is by far the richest gift of this character ever presented to a battleship or cruiser. The fund for the purchase and presentation of this service was conducted under the auspices of the *Indianapolis News*, one of the most progressive newspapers in the United States."

GLOUCESTER AND INDIANA .vs. THE SPANISH TORPEDO-BOAT
DESTROYERS

Lieutenant-Commander Richard Wainwright, who commanded the converted yacht Gloucester during the war, gives some details of the part taken by that vessel as she fought close by the Indiana in the battle with Cervera's fleet on July 3d, in a volume in the Library of Universal History dealing with the Spanish-American War. The following extracts are reprinted here, as relating to the Indiana's part in that action :

" The fleet opened fire at once on the Maria Teresa. We were heading out and commenced firing with our after guns. Our helm was put hard a-port, so that we turned toward the Indiana and in the direction taken by the enemy, and was kept a-port until we were heading at right angles to their column.

" The enemy soon developed their tactics, such as they were. They evidently expected to take advantage of their high speed and escape past the western end of our fleet before we could destroy them.

" We of the Gloucester closed in toward the enemy, firing such guns as we could bring to bear. We were near the Indiana and anxiously looking for the destroyers.

" As soon as the Pluton and Furor made their appearance our duty was plain—we must prevent them from attacking one of our battleships. We started ahead at full spead and gradually closed in on them, firing as rapidly as possible. About this time we made out a signal from the Indiana to read :

"' GUNBOATS CLOSE IN.'

" I have since heard that Captain Taylor intended to signal ' Torpedo boats coming out.' * To close in on the torpedo boats required us to cross the Indiana's line of fire, and as she was pouring in shell from her secondary battery, we were glad to feel secure that she would stop as we crossed her line."

---

* The signal made by the Indiana was, about 9.45 A.M. : " Enemy's torpedo-boats escaping or coming out to westward."

www.ingramcontent.com/pod-product-compliance
Lightning Source LLC
Chambersburg PA
CBHW030307170426
43202CB00009B/898